Philip Vera Cruz

Philip Vera Cruz

A Personal History

of Filipino Immigrants

and the

Farmworkers Movement

CRAIG SCHARLIN

LILIA V. VILLANUEVA

THIRD EDITION

With a New Foreword by Elaine H. Kim

UNIVERSITY OF WASHINGTON PRESS

Seattle and London

Originally published by the UCLA Labor Center and the UCLA Asian American Studies Center in 1992. Third edition published by the University of Washington Press in 2000. New Foreword by Elaine H. Kim copyright © 2000 by the University of Washington Press.

Library of Congress Cataloging-in-Publication Data

Scharlin, Craig.
    Philip Vera Cruz : a personal history of Filipino immigrants and the
    Farmworkers movement / Craig Scharlin and Lilia V. Villanueva; with a new
    foreword by Elaine Kim.—3rd ed.
        p. cm.
    Includes bibliographical references.
    ISBN 0-295-97984-4 (alk. paper)
    1. United Farm Workers—History.   2. Agricultural laborers—Labor
    unions—United States—History.   3. Alien labor, Philippine—United
    States—History.   4. Vera Cruz, Philip, 1904–1994.   I. Villanueva, Lilian V.
    II. Title.

HD6515.A292 U547 2000   331.88'13'092—dc21
    [B]   00-029902

The paper used in this publication is acid-free and recycled from 10 percent post-consumer and at least 50 percent pre-consumer waste. It meets the minimum requirements of American National Standard for Information Sciences—Permanence of Paper for Printed Library Materials, ANSI Z39.48-1984.

Personal history is one means by which
the politics of the recent past can be made relevant
to present history. —CAREY MCWILLIAMS

Contents

Foreword

Buried lives. We all know that history is usually a story told by its "winners." We learn about the Great Wall from the perspective of the Chinese monarchs, not from the viewpoints of the nameless peasants whose worn out and discarded bodies lie buried along its curves. Several years ago, Imelda Marcos, wife of the former and late Philippine president, wanted a palatial exhibition hall built in Manila in a hurry for an international film festival she was sponsoring. When part of the building collapsed, burying some laborers beneath it, she would not allow their bodies to be recovered. Instead, she ordered that construction be continued so that the event could be implemented as planned. Ironically, the event was poorly attended, and the exhibition hall has not been much used since. Some say that it is haunted by the ghosts of the workers who were sacrificed to it.

In the recent Hollywood film *The Sixth Sense*, the young main character sees ghosts that are invisible to everyone else. It may be that we Americans are also surrounded by ghosts. Occasionally archaeologists and construction companies unearth the bones of Native people who inhabited this land, of nameless slaves, coolies, and peons whose unrecognized labor made America rich. How many people have lived, labored, and died without leaving any record of their existence, not even a scribbled trace? Today, for the most part, we do not know who built the roads and bridges we travel; the buildings where we work, reside, and shop; the water and sewer systems we use daily. We don't usually think about who made our furniture and clothing, let alone our toothbrushes, nor about who tends, harvests, and transports the food we eat every day.

Philip Vera Cruz calls forth into cultural memory some of the people who have made American life possible, shining floodlights into dark corners and unearthing layer upon layer of buried stories—not just stories of workers, but stories of racialized Asian and Latino immigrant agricultural workers and the complex and little-discussed difficulties of multi-racial organizing.

An American story. I never actually met any Filipino Americans until I came to California in 1968, although I had heard about them from my parents, especially my mother, who had worked in the California fields herself. I remember her saying that when she was growing up, East and South Asians, Filipinos, Mexicans, and African Americans were restricted to movie theater balconies and not permitted to use public swimming pools except on the day before the pools were to be cleaned.

Shortly after arriving in the Bay Area, I attended a meeting of Women for Peace in San Francisco because I wanted to be involved in the movement against the U.S. war in Vietnam. It happened that Larry Itliong and another man from the United Farm Workers union were there, soliciting support for their lettuce boycott. I remember being surprised that they seemed so happy to see another Asian face in the room. Back then, especially for those of us who grew up on the East Coast, being Asian was simply an unfortunate disadvantage to be overcome or compensated for. It felt odd to be treated as though being Asian was a good thing. I learned much later that these Filipino farm labor leaders were accustomed to thinking in terms of ethnic alliances and collectivities.

Though they grew up in the Philippines, men like Larry Itliong and Philip Vera Cruz lived quintessentially American lives, inhabiting innumerable rural and urban locales, working at the most crucial hubs of production, trying to put democracy into practice through labor organizing. Moving from the cantaloupe fields of Chula Vista to the canneries outside Anchorage, they worked alongside people of many different racial and ethnic backgrounds. They were veterans of some of America's most spectacular labor movement activities on the plantations of Hawaii and in the fields and canneries of the Pacific Coast.

For many today, the American farmworkers movement is synonymous with Cesar Chavez and Mexican immigrant labor. But it was Filipino workers who laid the groundwork for the UFW. "Whatever happened to the Filipinos in the union, or to the Filipino farmworkers in general, is a question you don't hear being asked or read about in books about the farmworkers movement or the UFW," Philip Vera Cruz observes, "But . . . it's a question worth asking" (pp. 87–88).

Lateral lines. Before the demise of the USSR or the "evil empire," many Americans accepted the commercial news media's "good guys/bad guys" view of history and dualistic simplifications of the complex and layered relationships among diverse communities: majority/minority, mainstream/margin, native/immigrant, white/non-white. American life was a black/white story, with racialized people of many backgrounds swept into the black category. Historically, the central figure in the story was a white American. Even in today's more tolerant environment, people of color, if they appear at all, are the faceless crowds that constitute the exotic backdrop, the faithful servants who drive Miss Daisy, and the helpful sidekicks with no lives and hopes of their own. Even Hollywood films about slavery (*Amistad*), the Civil Rights movement (*Mississippi Burning*), or the Japanese internment (*Come See the Paradise* and *Snow Falling on Cedars*) center on the white characters. Likewise, most studies about "race relations" have been about a particular racialized group's relationship to whiteness or white society.

Americans of color share long, complex, and little-discussed relationships reminiscent of the relationships between villages linked by colonizers' roads—not to each other but to the sea, from which natural resources were taken and into which manufactured goods were pumped. The political, economic, and cultural histories of Mexico and the Philippines have much to share, but the discussion, instead of being direct, has been siphoned through the United States and Spain. Likewise, there are many parallels between Asian Indian and Korean American histories rendered invisible by British, Japanese, and American narratives. And unlike the assimilationist attempt to study Japanese-Anglo interracial marriages in recent decades, a long history of Chinese-Native American, Filipino-Native American, Filipino-Mexican, Sikh-Mexican, Chinese-African American, and indeed Japanese-Filipino and Chinese-Korean intermarriage was simply swept aside and ignored, so that we know about it mostly from our own experiences or from stories the old-timers tell us.

For the past several years, pundits have been talking about "the browning of America." It already seems that demographic shifts are resulting in more attention being paid to lines of affinity and difference among and within various ethnic and racial groups. We need to unearth the buried history of conflicts and coalitions among these groups. For instance, Afro-Asian friendship has hidden roots in our society. No one talks much about how people of the African American community stood, practically alone and certainly at no direct gain to themselves, against the abrogation of Japanese Americans' civil rights during World War II. Or how three-quarters of a century ago the mostly black Brotherhood of Sleeping Car Porters issued a public statement of solidarity with Filipino workers who, they said, "have been used against the unionization of Pullman porters just as Negroes have been used against the unionization of white workers."[1]

Americans of color have a proud if subterranean legacy of working together to fight economic and social injustice. Since the nineteenth century, Chinese Americans fought every piece of discriminatory legislation, sometimes all the way to the Supreme Court. Indeed, Chinese and African court cases against segregation inspired and propelled each other forward over the decades. The spectacular pan-ethnic labor organizing activities between Japanese and Filipinos in Hawaii at the turn of the century and the cross-racial labor organizing between Japanese and Mexicans in California in the first decades of this century have provided a legacy for labor organizing taking place in various parts of the country today, such as the multiracial San Francisco hotel maids' strike in the early 1980s and the pan-Asian American boycott of the Jessica McClintock clothing company in the 1990s, which included many Asian American participants and was strongly supported by Latina garment workers. The movement beyond narrow nationalism was clearly seen several years ago in Los Angeles, when Korean Immigrant Workers Advocates (KIWA) organizers fought against the South Korea-based corporation that acquired the Radisson Plaza Hotel and planned to replace unionized Latino workers with cheaper, non-unionized immigrant workers. Today, it is evidenced in the work of Asian American women involved in the San Diego-based movement against exploitation of women workers at Korean and Japanese-owned *maquiladoras* across the border with Mexico.

While it is important to divest ourselves of the old dominant-versus-marginal binary thinking, we have to resist the temptation to view relationships among racialized groups through rose-colored glasses. We will not be prepared for a new future if we ignore conflicts and differences. We have to scrutinize and understand anti-black prejudice among other people of color, anti-immigrant sentiment among African Americans and U.S.-born Asians and Latinos, exploitation of Asian and Latino undocumented immigrants by Asian and Latino employers, domination of smaller and poorer groups by larger and more powerful ones. Philip Vera Cruz's forthright and thoughtful account of what happened to Filipino farm workers in the UFW under Cesar Chavez is an important lesson about hegemony, about how one subordinated group can become subject to another and why it's important to protest and struggle even when some goals and concerns are shared.

The importance of Filipinos in Asian American history. Among Asian and Pacific Americans, Filipinos are unique because they share cultural space with both Latinos and East and Southeast Asian Americans. At the same time, they occupy a central place in Asian American history, which has been shaped by labor exploitation and U.S. imperialist wars in Asia. The U.S. national narrative disavows the fact of American military, economic, and cultural colonization of the Philippines, Korea, or Vietnam, but the immigrants' return to the imperial center to speak back from their very different positionalities, challenging racial categories and hierarchies, bringing back buried stories and images, disturbing the smooth silences that obscure ghosts and subjugated knowledges, contradicts and destabilizes America's fictions about itself.

Philip Vera Cruz's story bridges early and recent Asian American history, in terms of both the labor exploitation and U.S. political domination in Asia, which have differed in form rather than in substance during the past century. Vera Cruz's consciousness emerged from his participation in the Filipino *manongs'* agricultural labor movement that

spanned the decades from the 1920s to the 1980s, when he actively opposed the U.S.-supported Marcos dictatorship and pressed for an end
to martial law in the Philippines.

Global capitalist developments have brought flexible accumulation
practices, mixed production systems, and multiple sites of economic
opportunities in countries all over Asia and the Pacific, with profound
effects on Asian and Pacific migration and diaspora. As old concepts of
nationhood and the geographical boundaries around Asian and Pacific
workers melt away under the powerful search lights of global capitalism, sites of potential exploitation have become more diverse. In the
1990s and at the turn of the century, Asian and Pacific women are working on electronics assembly lines in both Asia and America and doing
piece work at home as well as toiling in garment factories, sometimes as
virtual slaves, like the Thai workers in El Monte, California, and sometimes in indentured servitude, as in Saipan, the American island of sweat-
shops. Today, the technology industry is avoiding the cost of training
and maintaining permanent workers in the United States by sending
work to cheaper skilled laborers in India and by sponsoring skilled workers from South Asia as temporary or "rotating labor" in this country. In
recent years, Silicon Valley's famed high-tech empire has displaced the
fields and orchards of the Santa Clara Valley where farmworkers like
Philip Vera Cruz once toiled. Who knows? Perhaps like the peasants who
built the Great Wall or the laborers crushed under the collapsing Philippine exhibition hall, they are ghosts whose bones lie buried, in this
case beneath the glass and steel buildings that are the future's new "factories in the field."

What has always been most impressive to me about Filipino Americans is the leading role they have taken in struggles for justice, both in
the labor movement in the United States and in the movement for democracy in the Philippines. They have provided inspiring models for
other Asian Americans to follow. Philip Vera Cruz is such a model, himself an embodiment of the spirit of caring about community that comes
from an understanding of history and appreciation of the world beyond
and from his compassionate but critical reflection in an age of celebrity

and materialism. Embracing his spirit of caring and interest in community, perhaps we can also dedicate ourselves to working towards a society that would recognize and reward all those whose labor and creative genius have given America its real greatness.

ELAINE H. KIM
University of California, Berkeley
January 2000

Introduction

Wen Manong: "Yes, Older Brother"

Among the Ilocanos of the northwestern Philippines, *Wen Manong* means respectfully listening to an elder during conversation. Ilocano was the language spoken by the majority of Filipino men who first arrived in America in significant numbers. It was the first language of Philip Vera Cruz. This phrase became a symbol of our commitment not only to listen to Philip's story, but also to remember those who came before us, to listen with respect to their stories and to learn from the past.

One hundred thousand Filipino men left the Philippines for Hawaii and the mainland United States during the first thirty years of the twentieth century. The earliest groups of these men were recruited to work in the sugar cane and pineapple fields of Hawaii. But many also made their way to the mainland, arriving primarily at the ports of Seattle and San Francisco, and found work on farms throughout California and the Pacific Northwest and in Alaska's canneries. Many eventually found their way into major metropolitan areas across the United States where they worked as menial laborers, such as busboys and bellhops, in restaurants and hotels and as domestic helpers. This book is about the life of one of these pioneering Filipinos in America, Philip Vera Cruz.

To understand why this group of Filipinos left their homeland in a major exodus to the United States, it is useful to look at the close relationship that developed between the Philippines and the United States from the time of the Spanish-American War in 1898 when the United States took over colonial rule of the Philippines from Spain. A very heated debate took place across the United States as to just exactly what role, if any, the country should play in the Philippines. Although the United States was just emerging as a world power, it had a long history of isolationism and anti-colonial attitudes were strongly felt. To become a new colonial power was not an easily acceptable idea for many Americans at the time.

At the height of the debate in the U.S. Congress over just what the U.S. relationship to the Philippines should be, President McKinley purportedly knelt down in his White House bedroom late one night to pray for guidance. As the story goes, he claimed to have received a reply from God that it was America's "Manifest Destiny" to take care of its "little brown brother," the Filipino. The actual validity of this story may be questionable but there is no doubt that the attitude it embodied ended up being the guiding force behind American policy toward the Philippines. This policy was carried out with an American zeal, continuously championed by the newly emerging American ethic that whatever is good for America is good for the rest of the world. The Filipinos, in effect, became the early recipients of the first massive American-styled colonization program. One hundred years of association with the United States, colonial and post-independence periods, have left a powerful imprint on the culture, lifestyle, and psyche of the Filipino people.

With U.S. colonial rule came American administrators and businessmen. American educators and missionaries also descended upon the Philippines to help "Americanize" the archipelago. As early as 1900, thousands of Filipino children were already being educated through the U.S.-styled free public school system established by American authorities throughout the country. The introduction of universal public education was one of the cornerstones of American colonial policy. Along with the new public school system came the introduction of the English language as the medium of instruction. The adoption of English was the master stroke of American colonization because "any Filipino who wanted employment or [sought] to get ahead was forced to learn the language. Opportunities for employment in government and in American firms were based on competence in English. From 1911 on, English became the official language of the courts."[1] With the use of American textbooks, "Filipinos began learning not only a new language but a new culture. Education became miseducation because it began to de-Filipinize the youth, taught them to look up to American heroes, to regard American culture as superior to theirs and American society as the model par excellence for Philippine society. The new textbooks gave them a good dose of American history while distorting, or at least ignoring, their own."[2] Benigno Aquino, Sr., father-in-law of former Philippine President Corazon C. Aquino and a pre-eminent spokesperson for independence during his time, remarked in 1928 on the use of the English language in Philippine society:

> To my mind one of the tragedies of present-day thinking in this country is the desire to use our general plan of public instruction as an instrument for the Americanization of our customs, our mannerisms, and our way of expressing ourselves. Even our hearts are now speedily beating and our souls sighing in the Anglo-Saxon way.[3]

It is not surprising then that the most notable book written by one of the early Filipino immigrants to the United States, Carlos Bulosan, was aptly titled *America Is in the Heart* (University of Washington Press, Seattle, 1973). It was only natural that Filipinos would soon start making the reverse trip across the Pacific to take advantage of the better educational and economic opportunities that were purported to be waiting for them in their benefactors' home country.

Filipino laborers first started to leave their country as early as 1906, partially through the recruitment efforts of the Hawaiian Sugar Planters Association (HSPA), to work in the sugar cane and pineapple fields of Hawaii. The immigration of Filipino laborers was slow for the first few years. By 1909 only a few hundred Filipinos had actually been recruited by the HSPA. More significant numbers did not start to arrive in Hawaii until after 1910 following the signing in 1907 of the Gentlemen's Agreement between the United States and Japan, which restricted the availability of Japanese workers as a cheap labor force in the Hawaiian fields.

The large influx of Filipinos to the American mainland started in 1924, the same year a major strike of the Hawaiian fields by Filipino workers, led by Filipino labor leader Pablo Manlapit, crippled the Hawaiian plantations. Following the strike many Filipino workers were blacklisted from the Hawaiian fields and their search for work on the mainland began. In addition to labor disputes in Hawaii, the U.S. Immigration Act of 1924, which barred Asian (primarily Chinese and Japanese) immigration, caused West Coast farmers and canneries to turn to Filipinos as a valuable alternate source of labor. Filipinos were a perfect group to fill this void since they were exempt from the exclusionary policies of the act because of their status as "U.S. nationals." By 1930 about a hundred thousand Filipinos, almost exclusively single men, were living in Hawaii and the mainland United States.[4]

Although Filipino laborers were actively sought by West Coast farmers and cannery operators, many American labor organizations, including the American Federation of Labor, were against this influx of foreign workers, arguing that like the Chinese and Japanese before them, "the Filipino had acted like a cancer in American private and public life, destroying American ideals and preventing the development of a nation based on racial unity."[5]

In 1934 the U.S. Congress passed the Tydings-McDuffie Independence Act. This act called for the Philippines to establish a constitutional form of government copied after the American prototype. The Philippines was to be granted its independence following a ten-year interval of preparatory "self-rule." The Tydings-McDuffie Act changed the status of all Filipinos from "U.S. national" to "alien," which quickly turned off the steady flow of Filipino migration. The U.S. Congress, concerned about high unemployment in the 1930s and sympathetic to the fears of conservative U.S. labor unions, argued that foreign workers were taking away jobs from white workers. In 1935, Congress passed the Filipino Repatriation Act, which offered mainland Filipinos free transportation back to the Philippines.[6] Although only a small number of Filipinos took advantage of the offer and returned to the Philippines, the passage of the act reflected a recurring bias in American society against foreign workers and in this case, Filipinos.

Not all of the Filipinos in the United States during this period came as laborers. Prior to 1920, around five thousand Filipino men attended American universities and colleges through the U.S. Pensionado Act of

1903. Under the Act, promising young Filipino men were selected for special education and training and then returned to work in the Philippines as industrial leaders, public school administrators, teachers, and government bureaucrats. These students were known as "the fountain pen boys." They returned to well-paying positions in the Philippines and their success stories inspired many young Filipinos to seek similar opportunities through an American education.

Philip Vera Cruz arrived in the United States in 1926. Although he came to earn a better living to help support his family in the Philippines, he also aspired to be a part-time fountain pen boy. Like many of his peers he believed in the American dream of success through better education. Tutored by American teachers and missionaries on the advantages of an American lifestyle and driven by the poverty of their rural upbringing, leaving for the promises of America was a natural conclusion for thousands of Filipino men at that time. To many provincial Filipinos, Hawaii and the mainland United States became meshed into their consciousness as one illusory windmill that appeared too wonderful not to pursue.

We met Philip Vera Cruz for the first time in Delano, California, in 1974 when we joined a group of student volunteers to help in the construction of the United Farm Workers' Agbayani Village, the union's retirement complex for elderly farmworkers. Delano, and for that matter most of the surrounding San Joaquin Valley of central California, is home to the "factories in the fields," a phrase coined by historian Carey McWilliams. The industrial style of farming perfected in the San Joaquin Valley has helped define the term "agribusiness."

This vast agricultural area is not a bucolic farm landscape. There are no rolling green hills, quaint farmhouses, red barns, or picturesque villages. It was once a vast desert, transformed into an agricultural megafactory only when water was brought in by massive state and federally funded irrigation projects in large man-made cement canals from the water-rich, green and lush, northern parts of the state. The sun can bake the valley in the summer to temperatures up to 115 degrees Fahrenheit.

With the introduction of a large and regular water supply, irrigating the already mineral rich soil, a multi-billion-dollar-a-year agricultural industry thrives. The farms and ranches throughout the valley are so vast, the land so flat, that as you gaze into the horizon, your line of sight only dissolves into the industrial haze, a by-product of large-scale farming. The San Joaquin Valley is the single most productive agricultural region in the world. The farming industry there has required large numbers of manual laborers to maintain the vast fields and keep the food products rolling to the markets of California, the United States, and the world. In this valley many of the old-timer Filipinos, the *manongs*, lived out the rest of their lives as retired farmworkers, most of them single and without families.

On our first visit to Delano and Agbayani Village we met and talked with many of the elderly Filipinos, Philip Vera Cruz among them. As second vice-president of the United Farm Workers (UFW) he was in charge of overseeing the volunteer work on the village. He took us around and introduced us to many of his friends. We made our first visit to the labor camps, home still to elderly Filipino farmworkers, many of them well past the age of normal retirement. The camps we visited were on private property and isolated from main highways and cities. The living conditions were crude. The rooms were extremely small with cracked walls stuffed with newspapers; the shower stalls, toilets and cooking facilities were open to the outside elements; the hallways too narrow for two people to pass. A Filipino old-timer who lived in one of these camps told us that the living conditions in his camp were basically the same as they were fifty years ago when he first arrived, fresh off the boat from the Philippines and full of high hopes. What made these Filipinos' situation most ironic was that they left their home country in search of better opportunities and half a century later their living conditions in the United States were not much better than those of tenant farmworkers living today in the Philippines. For many of them these camps had been the only home they had lived in since they arrived in the United States.

There is a tragedy associated with these men that contradicts the

American dream. They came to the United States not only believing in the American dream as other immigrants had, but unlike most others, they came already immersed in the best American democratic principles. Upon arriving in America, however, the Filipino soon discovered that his familiarity with American culture did not always work to his advantage. Being the most comfortable in America compared to other Asian immigrants, the Filipino was often regarded by Anglo Americans as arrogant and too fun loving for a newly arrived foreigner. The Filipino's preference for flashy clothes and bravado in dating white women only earned him the reputation of being racy and loose. What the Filipino had learned in the Philippines about equality and justice from American teachers did not translate into reality in the United States. Their reality was finding joy in poolrooms and dance halls, beauty and pride in personal grooming and clothes in an attempt to add flavor to a life that was all too often full of tragedy and resignation to a single life without much hope of starting their own family.

Almost all of the early Filipino immigrants came to the United States as single men. They did not come as most immigrants, seeking to make a new home for themselves. They came eager to take advantage of the U.S. job market and the American educational system to better prepare themselves to succeed back in the Philippines with its new Americanized social, cultural, and economic climate. They came as U.S. nationals free to enter and move around the United States with no intention of staying and making a new life in America. At the height of Filipino immigration, only a handful of Filipino women came to the United States. With the passing of the Tydings-McDuffie Independence Act of 1934, these men, numbering over a hundred thousand, became virtually cut off from future contact with women of their own nationality and generation. Most of these men remained without families in their old age, victims of restrictive immigration and anti-miscegenation laws.

National anti-miscegenation laws in the United States were originally passed to limit the mobility and constitutional rights of African Americans. These laws were later amended to include other non-whites when large groups of Asians arrived in the western states with the discovery of gold, the building of the transcontinental railroads, and the development of large-scale agriculture. In 1880, Section 69 of the California Civil Code was amended to prohibit the issuance of marriage licenses to whites and "Negroes and Mongolians." In 1931, Samuel Roldan, a Filipino who was denied a marriage license in Los Angeles, filed a lawsuit (Roldan v. Los Angeles County) charging that Filipinos, being Malay, did not belong to the Mongolian race. He won his case in the higher courts but the California Legislature hastily plugged the loophole in 1933 by adding the Malay race as one of those prohibited from marrying whites.[7]

A few Filipino men married white women by moving to states where such marriages were permitted, including Louisiana, New Mexico, and Nevada. However, when they returned to California, life was not easy for them. In *America Is in the Heart*, Carlos Bulosan describes what it was like for a Filipino who was married to a white woman at that time:

> One day a Filipino came to Holtville with his American wife and her child. It was blazing noon and the child was hungry. The strangers went into a little restaurant and sat down at a table. When they were refused service they stayed on, hoping for some consideration. But it was no use. Bewildered, they walked outside; suddenly the child began to cry with hunger. The Filipino went back to the restaurant and asked if he could buy a bottle of milk for his child. "It's only for the baby," he said humbly. The proprietor pushed him violently outside. "If you say that again in my place, I'll bash in your head!" he shouted aloud so that he would attract attention. "You goddamn brown monkeys have your nerve, marrying our women. Now get out of this town!"[8]

It wasn't until 1946 that the California Supreme Court ruled anti-miscegenation laws to be unconstitutional (Perez v. Sharp), and not until 1967 that the U.S. Supreme Court declared a similar ruling for the entire nation (Loving v. Virginia).

The Filipino old-timers came to this country as young men in search of good jobs with the intention of returning to their homeland and their families. But in the end, most of them could not return home. They became stranded in the harsh realities of the American economic system, unable to achieve the financial independence they dreamed of. And coupled with their strong sense of pride, returning home with only enough money to pay for passage seemed unacceptable. Most of these Filipino men eventually passed away alone, and they were, as Philip Vera Cruz told us in our early meetings, "a dying race."

During the second half of the 1960s and the early 1970s, the success of the farmworkers movement in California catapulted the United Farm Workers of America, AFL-CIO, and its charismatic leader, Cesar Chavez, into the limelight of the nation's labor struggles. Chavez's extraordinary success as a union organizer and leader resulted in the recognition of the UFW as a "Mexican" union. However, as Philip Vera Cruz points out, it is important to recognize that "other people have played important roles in the UFW too." Filipinos have been the dominant minority within that union. Unfortunately, being a "minority within a minority," the Filipinos' role and contributions to the farmworkers movement of the "Chavez" era have been mostly overlooked.

Filipinos actively participated in the farm labor movement in Hawaii and on the West Coast for over eighty years. They became prominent in the early 1920s when Pablo Manlapit led successful strikes in the Hawaiian fields. Filipino union organizers such as Chris Mensalvas, Ernesto Mangaoang, and Larry Itliong continued to play active and important roles in organizing Filipino farmworkers and addressing their needs. And it was, after all, the Filipino farmworkers, and not the Mexicans as is more commonly believed, who with courage and unity sat down in the grape fields of Delano, California, in 1965 and began the strike that became the impetus for the most successful chapter in the long history of farm labor struggles in California. There is an historical void regarding the role of Filipinos in this important labor movement. Filling that void can help better our understanding of all those involved in the farmworkers movement.

Philip Vera Cruz served as second vice-president of the UFW from the union's conception until his resignation in 1977. He was the highest-ranking Filipino officer of the UFW. Before serving in the UFW he was an officer of the Agricultural Workers Organizing Committee (AWOC), AFL-CIO, one of the two predecessor unions to the UFW. Despite the leadership positions he held, Philip Vera Cruz repeatedly acknowledged throughout the interviews his own shortcomings as a labor leader and often admitted that he failed to become the labor leader the Filipino farmworkers needed. However, he served in positions of official capacity within the farmworkers movement out of a genuine concern and commitment to improve the working and living conditions of not only the Filipinos but of all his fellow workers. His long involvement in the farmworkers' struggle gained him an international reputation as a committed labor leader of the highest integrity. Even his detractors showed respect for the strength of his convictions and the probity of his actions.

At the height of the popularity of the UFW and especially Cesar Chavez it was almost taboo among supporters to hear of any criticism of Cesar or the union. It was as if it were sacrilegious to look at the union or Cesar with anything but a supportive eye. And for Philip Vera Cruz the issue of criticizing UFW policies and specifically the leadership of Cesar Chavez was one of great concern and often quite troubling. Although there were a number of key and very heated debates within the union he never publicly aired his differences with Cesar or the union leadership while he was an officer of the UFW. This was difficult, but he felt it was a principle he could not break. He couldn't have felt more strongly about the importance of keeping in-house disputes in house, no matter how much he realized this limited his ability to communicate truthfully about union matters.

It was only after Philip resigned from union leadership that he felt free to express his positions and attitudes on a number of controversial issues regarding the UFW. In this book, Philip Vera Cruz discusses openly and candidly his past differences with the union leadership. He does so with care and introspection and emphasizes the importance of presenting all sides of an issue so that intelligent and responsible analysis of the events may be rendered. As he often stated, he felt very strongly that "we need the truth more than we need heroes."

Introduction

Philip Vera Cruz's oral biography can be seen as a collection of stories that are parables on correct versus incorrect conduct. He was a highly ethical person who constantly asked: "What is the moral and correct thing to do to be a good person and at the same time be good to my fellow human beings?" He didn't just tell us stories about his life, he also questioned the actions of those in the story, be it relations between parents and child, siblings, friends and co-workers. He didn't just observe the politics of the UFW but also deliberated on the actions of the organization on ethical and moral grounds. In his observations about the UFW he analyzed not only the conduct of the rank and file union members but also the actions of its leaders, be they Mexican, Filipino or Anglo.

American historian William Appleman Williams, in his book *The Contours of American History*, writes that history is a way of learning when "it can offer examples of how other men faced up to the difficulties and opportunities of their eras. Even if the circumstances are noticeably different, it is illuminating and productive of humility as well, to watch other men make their decisions and to consider the consequences of their values and methods."[9] Philip Vera Cruz has opened his life to us in this personal memoir so we can broaden our historical view through his experiences. He firmly believed that "our survival in this country is determined by how well we learn from the lessons of the past." If it is true, as the eighteenth-century French naturalist Leclerc de Buffon once remarked, that "the style is the man himself,"[10] then Philip Vera Cruz has given us in this book a complete picture of himself. Like Philip Vera Cruz, this memoir is marked by restraint, conviction, caring, and sensitivity towards his fellow man.

We wish to express our sincere appreciation to the individuals who encouraged us to undertake this project and those who inspired us to its completion. Rodel Rodis, for inviting us to Agbayani Village and for introducing us to Philip; Debbie Vollmer, long time partner of Philip, for taking the best care of Philip; Kent Wong, Director of the UCLA Center for Labor Research and Education, for his enthusiasm and support of Philip and for his important contributions toward the publication of the first edition of this book; Glenn Omatsu, Russell Leong, Augusto Espiritu, and Mark Pulido, for their valuable assistance with the first and second editons of the book; Willa Baum, Director of Regional Oral History Office, University of California, Berkeley, also our friend and neighbor, for her support and encouragement over the years; Linda Nietes, for urging us to extend the life of the book; John Silva and Jonathan Best for their kind support and encouragement, and last but not least, Carey McWilliams, posthumously, for seeing the value of this work before anyone else did and who single-handedly provided the inspiration for us to complete this book.

We thank you all.

CRAIG SCHARLIN AND LILIA V. VILLANUEVA

Berkeley, California

January 2000

Philip Vera Cruz

Profits Enslave the World

While still across the ocean,
I heard about the U.S.A.,
So thrilled by wild imagination,
I left home through Manila Bay.

Then on my way I thought and wondered
Alone what would the future be?
I gambled parental care and love
In search for human liberty.

But beautiful bright pictures painted
Were just half of the whole story...
Reflections of great wealth and power
In the land of slavery.

Minorities in shanty towns, slums...
Disgraceful spots for all to see
In the enviable Garden of Eden,
Land of affluence and poverty.

Since then I was a hungry stray dog,
Too busy to keep myself alive...
It seems equality and freedom
Will never be where billionaires thrive!

A lust for power causes oppression
To rob the poor in senseless greed;
The wealthy few's excessive profits
Tend to enslave the world in need.

—*Philip Villamin Vera Cruz*[†]

"Still good at sitting down"

Delano, California, 1977. I have to clean out my office and move out. Since my resignation I have been ready to leave so it's not as if I don't want to. But this place does have its memories. It represents the farmworkers movement in the U.S. It's a symbol of our struggle. Yet what a pity that the union doesn't show more respect for it and has simply abandoned it, and let it get run-down like it is now. The land here is called Forty Acres, since that's the size of the lot. When you say "Forty Acres," there are people all over the world who know that you are talking about the United Farm Workers, Cesar Chavez, the farmworkers, the grape pickers. Forty Acres is really synonymous with the farmworkers movement, and the UFW which is the legal body of that movement. For twelve years Forty Acres was the home of the UFW.

Across the hall outside my office is the Hiring Hall where many famous meetings have taken place. Next door you can still find the Health Clinic. Outside the Hiring Hall at the other end of that dusty parking lot, which never got paved, is the gas station. It's funny how one gas station could become so famous. Everyone in Delano, and for that matter most of the San Joaquin Valley, knows that gas station. It belonged to the UFW, and it too was a symbol that farmworkers could organize their own lives and not always be at the mercy of oil cartels.

But like the offices, the Hiring Hall, and eventually the Health Clinic on Forty Acres, the gas station, too, is closed down, and it looks just like any other closed-down gas station. I guess whether a union or a large corporation closes down a gas station it looks about the same in the end.

And across the Forty Acres on the other side is Agbayani Village, the union's retirement home. It's about the only part of Forty Acres that has any life left in it and at that it's not much, just all the chickens, dogs, and of course, the *manongs*, the retired Filipinos, the old-timers, not doing much. I'm one of them though I don't live in the village like they do. I think it's sort of fitting that after Cesar and the UFW board members decided to abandon Forty Acres and move the union headquarters to La Paz in the foothills above Bakersfield, Forty Acres has been left mostly to Filipino old-timers. After all, it was the Filipinos, not the Mexicans, who started this phase of the farmworkers movement when they alone sat down in the Delano grape fields back in 1965 and started what became known as the "farmworkers movement" that eventually developed into the UFW. And now, here at Forty Acres, one of the symbols of that movement, just like that black eagle on the union's red flag, the only ones left are the Filipinos who are now too old to do much work, that's for sure, but still good at sitting down.

From the slum district near the northside and across the river in Chicago, I came and lived in the shanty towns of the San Joaquin Valley in California back in 1943. I started working in the grape vineyards early that spring and didn't stop picking grapes until the Delano grape strike in September 1965.

The first farm I worked at in Delano was the Martin Gutunich Farm on Driver Road, between Garces and Ninth Street. It was an 80-acre vineyard. After Martin Gutunich and his wife died, their children continued to work the land and Dispoto, a son-in-law, ran the business.

When there was no work at the Gutunich farms, some of the other Filipinos and I would often go to work on another ranch nearby hoeing cantaloupe. We weeded the plants in rows, the ground was very hard and it was hot too. I was not used to bending and working like that, having worked for many years at restaurants in big cities. I couldn't straighten my back for three or four days. It was so hard on me that I changed my mind about working in the fields and wanted to quit. When my back was really aching out in those hot fields, I often daydreamed about when I was a small boy in the Philippines. I'd remember how much I enjoyed those years when it was my job to tend the *carabaos* (water buffalos) because my father was not healthy and could not do that chore. Other men usually did that kind of work so I was almost always the only kid among a group of older men.

Vera Cruz's first job in the United States was as a busboy in the Royice Cafeteria, Spokane, Washington, 1927.

Philip Vera Cruz at the Spokane Country Club, where he worked between 1929 and 1932.

Studio portrait of Vera Cruz and coworkers in a box factory in Cosmopolis, Washington. Back row (left to right): Pedro de la Cruz, Philip Vera Cruz, Mariano Ballote, and Melchor Villa; front row (left to right): Felipe Argel, Arcadio Villa, Jose Sanchez, and Adriano Villa. All these men were related to Philip Vera Cruz, but they did not know of each other's presence in the United States until they met by accident in Cosmopolis.

Filipino cabbage pickers in California. Photo by Dorothea Lange; courtesy of the Library of Congress, LC-USI62 119854

West Coast hotel, early 1930s. Courtesy Visual Communications Archives, Los Angeles

Philip Vera Cruz as an organizer for the Agricultural Workers Organizing Committee, 1965.

Philip Vera Cruz participated in debates held regularly in Chicago's Filipino community between 1934 and 1942.

Filipino laborers return from work in an agricultural field in Stockton, California, in the 1930s. Courtesy Visual Communications Archives, Los Angeles

Formative years of the United Farm Workers; Philip Vera Cruz at far right. UFW headquarters, Delano, California

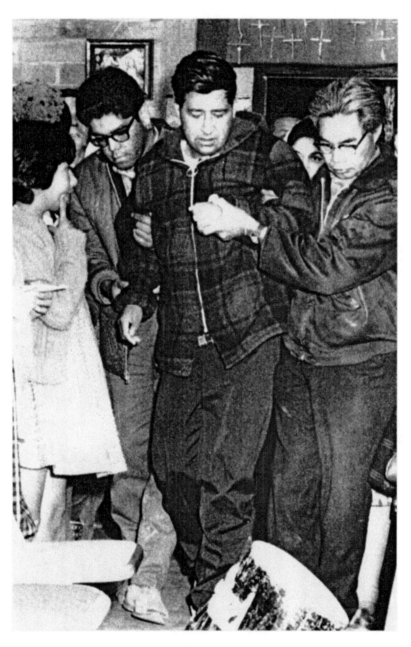

Weakened by a three-week fast, Cesar Chavez is helped to a Mass in his honor.
Philip Vera Cruz (right) holds Chavez's arm. UPI

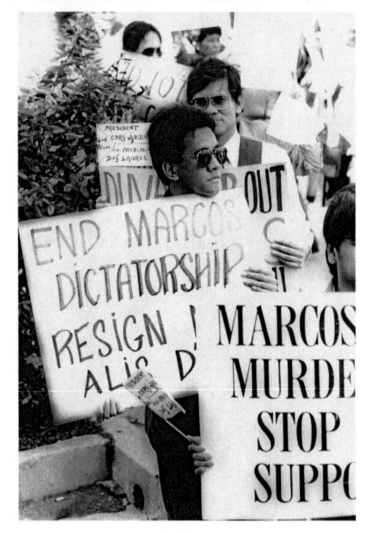

Opposite, top: In the early and mid-1970s, Filipino Americans and Filipino expatriates rallied against the dictatorship of Ferdinand Marcos in the Philippines. These demonstrations—held in cities across the United States—raised public awareness of the political situation in the Philippines. Courtesy Visual Communications Archives, Los Angeles

Opposite, bottom: The beginnings of Agbayani Village in Delano, California, in the early 1970s. Courtesy Visual Communications Archives, Los Angeles

Philip Vera Cruz at Agbayani Village, Delano, California, 1975. Photo by Craig Scharlin

Philip Vera Cruz at his home. Photo by Craig Scharlin

I remember that when it rained we all wore a native raincoat made of *nipa* leaves tied together with a hole for the neck. It went straight down to the knees. *Nipa* is the same material used to make roofs of native Filipino houses. It worked very well as a roof or as a coat because the rain could never penetrate through *nipa*.

I remember the men huddled together in the rain, watching their *carabaos*, smoking, and telling stories to each other. Some would be perched on top of their *carabaos*, because when it rained, the animals released steaming body heat and provided its rider with a natural heater. Sometimes the group would squat under a tree or some kind of shelter, their *nipa* raincoats sticking out horizontally. I looked like a turkey with its back feathers spread out when I wore one of those *nipa* raincoats. The older men also wore hats on rainy days which were made from shells of dried *opo*, which is a kind of gourd. It was a protection for the head as well as for tobacco during the rain-watch days. There were built-in compartments inside those hats which were ideal for storing tobacco and matches. It was very handy because the heat from the head kept the matches dry and easier to light.

When I was young, we didn't have watches or clocks around. Nature was our timekeeper. We could tell pretty well when it was noontime and time for lunch because the sun would be right above our heads. But in the evening it was harder to guess the time. So we relied on two small plants, the *andadasi* and *mimosa*, which were all over the place. You see, these plants would close their leaves when there was not enough sunlight. We used this sign as our time guide: when the plant closed up, it meant it was already dark enough and therefore time to go home. Even during rainy days, those plants closed up at sunset. Those were easy and relaxed times for me taking my father's place on the *carabao* watch. It was pleasurable work, not backbreaking like my farm jobs in Delano.

When I started working in Delano, I lived in labor camps on the farms, as most workers did, especially the Filipinos because we were mostly single men without families. The facilities in those camps were pretty bad. The first camp I lived in had a kitchen that was so full of holes, flies were just coming in and out at their leisure, along with mosquitoes, roaches, and everything else. You didn't have to know much about sanitation not to want flies on your plate. The toilet was an outhouse with the pit so filled-up it was impossible to use. The grower didn't even care to have another hole dug until the workers complained. I remember the grower saying, "Well damn it, dig another hole!," when we brought up our complaint. So we dug a new hole ourselves.

After this episode I decided maybe farmwork wasn't for me and thought about going back to the city. But I had to wait because of the condition of my back. My backache from working in the fields certainly proved wrong a popular saying among racist growers that the Filipinos made good farm workers because they were short and built close to the ground, making it easier for them to bend over. Shit. I'm a short Filipino but it was just as hard for me to bend over as any big white guy. Some of those growers didn't even know how difficult it was out there, bending over with the sun beating down on you. I was new at the work, of course, but nevertheless, it was a backbreaking job.

I waited around for my back to heal, and when it did, my Uncle Sabino, who lived in Delano and was a first cousin of my father, told me of a job on a farm that was easier. He said, "Why don't you try it? Maybe you'll like it." So I went to this farm and the job was O.K. My back got stronger and stronger and pretty soon I was working and doing harder jobs. The thought of going back to the noise of the city made me like the farm better, so I stayed. In retrospect, I realize that deciding to stay on the farm in Delano was like completing a full cycle of my life.

I was born on Christmas Day, 1904, in a small barrio called Saoang, in the province of Ilocos Sur, which is on the island of Luzon. Saoang is in the northwestern part of Luzon far north of Manila. There was a small port in Saoang where sailboats carried migrant workers from our area as far north as Cagayan and south to Pangasinan for rice planting and harvest. These workers would bring back their shares of the crop as wages at the end of the season. Most of the people of Saoang however farmed small pieces of land or fished for their food. Those who worked the land grew rice, corn, sugarcane, onions, just about anything that would grow. Although the land was good there wasn't much of it since the high mountains of northern Luzon came right down to the ocean. Saoang was the center of activities of just simple folks. Residents met each other as they rode their carts about town pulled by *carabaos* and oxen, some of them coming from nearby barrios to sell their goods.

I was born and raised in small rural towns in the Philippines and finally after leaving my home, crossing the Pacific in search of a better life, wandering around the U.S. for many years, I finally returned to a rural place, although Delano and the San Joaquin Valley are very different physically from my home town in the Philippines. Saoang was green, lush, tropical; it was always humid, and there was always the sight of the blue ocean that contrasted so beautifully with the rolling green foothills that came down almost to the water, whereas Delano is flat, hot but dry, with almost no green vegetation except what's planted on the farms, and no bodies of water.

❧

When I decided to stay in California I guess I was unconsciously carrying on the Saoang tradition of migrant work, for when the grape season was over in Delano we would work on lettuce in nearby MacFarland and Wasco or pack grapes for growers in other areas. I also thinned plums in Arvin-Lamont, cut raisin grapes in Selma, or asparagus in Byron. Our pay then was about 70 cents an hour, eventually going up to 80 cents. We usually worked a nine-hour day but during the busy times we worked ten hours a day. That was in the 1940s.

Wherever else I worked, I always returned to Delano, which became my real home. I didn't exactly choose to live in Delano, it was more a matter of circumstances that placed me there. In fact, before I went to Delano, I had never even heard of the place.

In August of 1942, I got drafted and was immediately sent to San Luis Obispo, California, for basic training. I was assigned to the second Philippine Infantry which was sent on to Camp Cook. Those of us over 38 years old were then discharged and assigned to jobs on the farms in the

San Joaquin Valley or in the shipyards up north in Vallejo and other defense-related industries. Through a cousin of my father I bumped into while in camp, I found out about another cousin of mine living in Delano who I decided to visit. I found out from him that the army was releasing many Filipinos to work on the farms, so I decided to join them.

Since I came to Delano at the beginning of the war, except for short periods of time here and there, I have lived here longer than any other place in my life, including the Philippines.

Living in Delano from the early 1940s on, I discovered that there were all sorts of rackets going on. I really thought it was a very bad, very immoral place. Filipinos were constantly the victims of gambling joints and prostitution. Then again, those who were supposed to be leaders of the Filipino community were often gamblers themselves and when there was trouble these so-called community leaders would always side with the growers, city councilmen, police, and the city judge against their powerless fellow Filipinos.

At that time the town of Delano was divided by the railroad tracks which ran north and south. These tracks also served as the color-line between the minority farmworkers and the white farmers. West of the tracks was Chinatown and pool halls that welcomed us non-whites while the town's business district, run mostly by whites and where we felt uncomfortable to walk around, was east of the tracks. The business area ran two-and-a-half blocks between 9th and 12th Avenues on Main Street. There was a bank, a post office and a movie theater. All the buildings were small but quaint. The white farmers who lived out on their farms in the countryside came to this part of town once a week, filling up the sidewalks and flocking into the few stores. The parents brought their children, and I'm sure it was always an experience for the children after being out on the farm all week. For the children it was exciting but for me it was different. All the people who worked in these stores and all the shoppers were lily-white, and too many were arrogant and sarcastic towards Filipinos. You could always feel their sense of racial superiority.

The Delano Theater practiced racial segregation. Seats on the northside and in the center were reserved for whites only. A small part of the theater was for the minority grape pickers: Orientals, Mexicans, Blacks, Puerto Ricans, Arabs, and of course, the Filipinos.

Even the minorities didn't mix with each other back then. Nobody seemed to like anybody else very much except their own kind. And among us the attitude of some Filipinos towards their own people was often cold and indifferent. I remember the unpleasant feeling that would run through my spine when I saw acquaintances as they passed me by without the slightest sign of a friendly greeting. Maybe we had just talked before or even eaten at the same table at the labor camp but they would move past me in town as if we had never met. This attitude was quite prevalent among the minority workers then and it hurt no one but ourselves. There were many incidents where one Filipino had ripped off another, causing Filipinos to be suspicious of their own people. I learned quickly in this country that when people are poor and hungry they will turn even against their own. Real communication between minorities was very limited at that time because of strained personal relations. This was a very damaging attitude; it was a faint reflection of the pressures the minorities felt from the racist community. They were hesitant to mingle with their own in the presence of white folks.

On Saturdays and Sundays during the grape harvest season, the Filipinos who lived in labor camps would come to town and stay in and around Chinatown, west of the railroad tracks. That's because we really weren't welcome in other parts of town, didn't have any other place to go. We didn't do much, just hung around, and this sort of developed as a habit among the Filipino laborers, this hanging around Delano's Chinatown, and although times have changed, you can still see groups of Filipinos doing the same thing on Saturday and Sunday to this day.

Although our work was strenuous it was also monotonous, so after the day's work was done, we'd take quick showers, eat a hurried dinner, and all go into town and just hang-out, pace up and down on a one-block section of sidewalk. You'd see Filipinos walking slowly by a restaurant or a bar, going close to the window, screening their eyes to see inside, peeping through to see who was there. They seemed to be always looking for someone, some acquaintance or friend, but really I don't think there was usually anyone in particular on their mind.

There were always many farmworkers standing in groups talking about grapes: the names of the different growers, locations of the ranches, acreage, wages and bonuses, how much was taken out of their salary for board, hours of work, cooks—you know, who could cook this and that, who was a good cook, and whose cooking could almost kill you, or who cooked the real Filipino food. You know, stuff like that. The most important topic was always how the growers were, which ones were reasonable to work for. To get through the crowd, you had to take a detour or completely get off the sidewalk and walk right down the middle of Glenwood Street.

That sidewalk in Chinatown was the busiest employment service in Delano. It was an open hiring hall for Filipino grape pickers. A foreman, or anyone ordered by the grower to get an additional worker, would be sent, like a dispatcher, down to Glenwood Street in Chinatown. The Filipino's labor was always at the mercy of others. You could be hired in Chinatown but rejected when you reported on the job, or you could be accepted for work and then later fired without reason. Because of this unfair situation even the smallest landowners would often act like dictators. Right or wrong, wise or foolish, his word was law, he was the supreme court whose decision was absolute, and the Filipino just accepted this situation down there on Glenwood Street.

Many of my Filipino brothers were quite shy. They would just stand there watching the passers-by, sometimes looking to the north end of the buzzing sidewalk then turning to the south to see what was happening. Some of us would be squatting or sitting on copies of the *Delano Record* on the edge of the sidewalk. We must have looked like brown owls, you know, sitting there and occasionally turning our heads from one side to the other to check if the entire flock along the block was still at peace.

If you went into the restaurants, bars, card rooms, and pool halls, you would find them packed with Filipino grape pickers. Since the weekly workday was dreary and routine, this would give them a change of environment, and they didn't mind paying the high prices on the menu for food or for a beer at the bar. Some were so hungry for some interesting or at least different food that they were happy just to be busy eating. Others were just lingering around and flirting with the waitresses or girls behind the bar. The card rooms and pool halls were usually together and there were always women all over the place participating in all these activities. The whole business looked like a mixed-up affair, you know what I mean, poor minority farmworkers, poor white women, all hustling.

The Filipino man, because of his lowly position in society, due to ignorance or discrimination, was often getting taken, and all too often it was another poor woman, a white woman hustling, who would take him. There were no Filipino women around for us. Only men came over to the U.S. You have to remember that most of us came with no intention of staying forever, with no intention of making the U.S. our home. We had strong pride and as one year rolled into another it was hard for us to admit that we were stuck and were not going home, successful and ready to start and support a new family back in the Philippines. As our time in this country lengthened and our loneliness increased the Filipino man became very vulnerable to hustlers. The Filipinos were kind of weak when it came to women but they couldn't be blamed. It's only natural to be attracted to the opposite sex, especially white women. They were new and special, so different looking. Because of our colonial education we looked up to anything American as good. There was tremendous frustration among Filipinos in this country because of how difficult it was for them to raise a family. Anti-miscegenation laws made it illegal until the 1960s in the U.S. for a Filipino male to marry a white woman in several states, such as California and Illinois, where most of the Filipinos lived.

Sex, therefore, became a different sort of thing for the Filipino male, a cause for problems. But the laws of nature are very strong and often the Filipino man fell into the same trap over and over again. Filipinos, who were overly in need of a woman's love and companionship, and having a natural desire to help others who were also hard-up, were extremely vulnerable to be hustled by a poor white woman.

The story was all too familiar. A hustler would tell a guy she loved him to get his trust. And then pretty soon she would say to him something like, "Well honey, you can't read very well," or "you don't speak good English, so, why don't you put your car in my name. If something happens to your car and you might not understand, then I can go and take care of it while you're at work and you won't be bothered." Well, the next thing the guy would hear is that her mother was sick and she has to go see her but she'll be back soon. So the car is gone and maybe she is even writing for some more money. This story was all too common among my group of Filipino men.

When I was working at the W & R restaurant in Chicago, there was this guy Bennie who worked in the kitchen peeling potatoes, bussing dishes from the dining room to the kitchen and washing. Everyone called him "Hollywood" because he liked the movies, looked a little like some actor, and was also a flashy dresser. One day we were told that Hollywood was going to get married to a beautiful white girl. She was one of those dance hall girls and that's where Hollywood met her. She was very small, just like a small Filipino girl and very beautiful. Hollywood bought her a big ring which cost him more than he could afford. They got married but that same evening, right after the wedding, she told Hollywood that she was leaving him and going back to the dance hall. She left and just disappeared with the ring and some of the money. Nobody ever saw her again. For the next few days some of the guys in the kitchen were kidding Hollywood about it. They were laughing but Hollywood didn't answer and just kept working. Finally one of the guys said, "You know, brother, if you don't stop that, Hollywood is going to kill somebody." There was no incident that time in our kitchen, but you'd often hear stories about one guy who killed another in a situation like that, or of a suicide.

A Filipino as a poor but hard-working minority usually married another minority, usually a Mexican because they often lived in the same area. But if a Filipino wanted to marry a white woman, because of the anti-miscegenation laws, they would have to either go to Mexico or to another state to get married, and then when they came back they would often face tremendous discrimination not only from the white community but also from their own. As I said, their relationship often started because the Filipino would lend some money to help out the girl. But often a closer relationship would develop with a real love and respect for each other and soon they would get married. But because of his friends' experiences with white women hustlers, he and his wife were not always accepted by his own people right away. "She's another whore," or "Hmmm, another cheapy," that's how the Filipino community would view his new wife. This wasn't fair, of course, because even if she was a hustler, or even a prostitute, chances are inevitable circumstances made her that way and who's to say that she really didn't love the guy and would change her ways.

And of course the pressure from the white community was always there for both the Filipino and his white bride. I know a white woman, a Jewish lady, who was growing up in Los Angeles in the 1920s and 30s and she told me recently that she remembers being told by some of her friends to stay away from those "monkeys," meaning the Filipinos, because they were dangerous and that they only hung around with bad women. Since Filipinos were looked down upon and were always poor, when the whites found someone of their own race going with a Filipino, then they, too, would prejudge that person and call her a cheapy or a prostitute even if it wasn't true.

It was always a difficult situation for the mixed couple who sincerely loved each other and because of outside pressures many marriages between Filipinos and white women were not successful. Racist legislation and attitudes in the U.S. denied my generation of Filipinos the right to raise a family like a normal human being. We became an entire generation that was forced by society to find love and companionship in dancehalls. I am not over-exaggerating when I say that my group of pioneering Filipinos is a dying race.

∽

Many Filipinos in Delano preferred going to pool halls, trying to look and feel important. A common sight in these places would be a Filipino entering and walking erectly, seemingly with dignity. He'd stop at the counter and survey the Havana cigars and probably fill his shirt pocket with those fat cigars. There was nothing more prestigious then; it really was the style then to have your pocket full of those Havana cigars. Then the poor grape picker would light up and smoke a big cigar in the corner of his mouth to get the feeling and semblance of being a prosperous grower or maybe even a banker. But he was really smoking to ease his nervousness or maybe just because he was addicted to that habit-forming stimulant.

I didn't like it in those pool halls but I can still remember the scene in there. Sputum from the tobacco juice spotted the floor along the walls, particularly heavy in the corners. There were always the gamblers in an adjoining room playing cards or dominos and their clouds of smoke would reflect off the lights. Many of those guys who sat there for several years, continually inhaling that foul air night after night, eventually made a sad and lonely trip to the tuberculosis sanitarium. For some it was their first and last trip. Those grape pickers ruined their health and many of them lost their lives from that environment and I believe that so much of it was the unnecessary but inevitable cruel effects of forced racial segregation.

Sometimes a squabble started in one of the card rooms. One guy got caught cheating in *paralasi*, or some game like that, and another player pulled a knife on him. The others then grabbed the guy with the knife to calm him down while the suspected cheater ran quickly out through the door, knocking down the men who were just sitting and talking out on the sidewalk. Before anyone knew it, the fight escalated and got worse, spilling into the streets with several people involved. The owner of the establishment called the Delano Police Department. Those proprietors of the gambling joints kept good relations with the city police so they could call on them to take care of whatever headaches roughnecks caused. The police arrived and mixed in with the crowd, now seemingly peaceful. Since the police were not sure who was involved in the

14

fight they arrested people randomly on the sidewalk. But before they left, the police chief delivered a stern lecture which went something like this: "You (meaning us Filipinos) are supposed to be in the labor camps to pick grapes where the growers need you. If you don't do that then go back to where you came from or I'll throw you all in jail. I don't want to see you here in town again." That may sound just like in the movies more than reality but that's really the way it happened. Of course it was illegal to gamble but no one tried to put a stop to it because it worked to the growers' advantage to keep Filipinos gambling for it kept them broke. This way the Filipino could not fight back or hold out during a labor dispute because they always needed the money. It was, you could say, some kind of a planned frame-up against the minority farmworkers. There were a lot of Filipino organizations in Delano then but unfortunately, most Filipino community leaders just took advantage of the situation. They chose to live off the rackets themselves, from the bars for the disgusted and the despondent, the gambling for the unjust and greedy and the dance halls for the lonely and the unhappy. These businesses were sources of easy but questionable money, and the proprietors always aligned themselves with the city council, police, and sheriff departments, and even some minority civic leaders to exploit the minorities in general.[1]

That was Delano then. But somehow, despite all this, I still wanted to stay in Delano rather than go back to the city. There weren't any good job opportunities waiting for me in the city, anyhow. Maybe if I had completed my education I could have gotten a special job as a mechanic or a teacher, but then, of course, there were no Filipino teachers in this country during those days. It would have been difficult because even if I had a skill I would still have been overlooked because I am a minority. My choices of jobs in the city were to be a dishwasher, busboy, or maybe work in a hotel. When you worked in a restaurant you had to go to work every day. If you missed one day you could get fired if you did not have a very good reason. Even though you usually would not get fired if you were sick for just a day, if you were sick for a long time then you'll definitely get fired. But in farmwork you can say you are not feeling well and not go to work. You'll be warned if you did that often, of course, but then you can always say, "To hell with them" and try and find work in another ranch or farm. There was more freedom on the farms, I thought. Also, it is cheaper to live in the country, although you can't make much money either.

Chicago was the only city I could have gone back to because that's where most of my friends had been. But a lot of them left Chicago during the war like I did so I figured that few, if any, of my friends would've been around if I went back there. Many got drafted into the army and I even saw some of them out here in California before they got shipped out.

In 1948 I went up to Stockton for the first time during the seasonal break from grapes in Delano to work in the asparagus fields. The farm I worked at was actually in Byron, a small town about seventeen miles north of Stockton, close to Highway 99. I went there with my second cousin, Fortunato Villamin, whose father was a cousin of my mother. We had a cousin in Byron who was then a foreman in a labor camp. His name was Ben Apostol. But Ben had changed his last name. At that time he was known as Ben Delbejes.

"How come you changed your name?" I asked him.

"Well," he said, "because when something goes wrong around here the police always want to pick me up." So that's why he had two names. It was not very common, but some Filipinos used several names because they had been arrested once, twice, or even three times before by the police for being in a brawl or something.

It was also common for Filipinos to use a nickname for their friends. It promoted a feeling of familiarity among us when we felt so much alienation from the society around us. But sometimes this pervasive use of nicknames caused problems. There was this guy I knew in Chicago and everybody called him "Racklous" because he worked at a Greek restaurant by that name. We never knew his true name because everyone always just called him Racklous. Well, one day someone came around asking for him by his real name and we all said, "Sorry, we don't know that guy." That's the way it was. There were all these guys that I knew only by their nicknames. It was as if many of us Filipinos were living behind hidden identities for fear of associating with the realities of our lives, our real names, and therefore, our real identities.

My cousin and I were in Stockton that year of the big Filipino strike in the asparagus fields. Fortunato and I joined the strike but Ben didn't want to because he was a foreman. He didn't want us to join the strike either so that created a conflict between us. But my cousin and I went on strike anyway, and our headquarters was on El Dorado Street in Stockton, a popular street among Filipinos. I was so naive that I didn't even know the name of the union organizing the strike, but I knew it was part of the CIO and that the leaders were Filipinos.

We were striking a wide area: Stockton, Elton, Byron, Tracy, and some other towns. It was really a big strike. You see, the asparagus plants have to be cut back everyday in order to keep them from growing tall and blooming. During the strike the owners used machines to cut their plants to save the part that's underground. They just left the cut pieces, the marketable asparagus, in the fields to rot. The strike, as I recall it, was over wages and better conditions at the camps, just the basics, you know. We were not even asking for pension, medical care, or even for a contract!

The most important memory I have of that strike was the leadership of Chris Mensalvas. He organized that strike along with his close friend Ernesto Mangaoang. Both were exceptionally good Filipino labor leaders and people should know more about them. Chris was probably the most outstanding Filipino union organizer in this country throughout the 1940s and 50s. Chris and Ernesto had gained so much prestige and success with labor organizing, that out of fear and outright collusion with the agricultural industry, the government even tried to discredit them. At that time, Chris was the president of the Cannery Workers Union, ILWU Local 37, and Ernesto was the business representative. They were popular with the workers because they were both very honest and able. Well, the government tried to deport them to the Philippines under the McCarran Act, claiming that they were aliens and communist agitators. But Chris and Ernesto won their case against the government after the U.S. Supreme Court ruled in *Mangaoang v. Boyd* that Filipinos who entered this country before 1936 entered as nationals and therefore, were not aliens. So they could not be deported. Filipinos were not considered aliens in the U.S. until after the Philippines declared its independence.

The Stockton strike was the first major agricultural workers strike after the war. The Delano strike in 1965 by the UFW was bigger in scale and impact, of course, but back then, especially for me, the Stockton strike was the biggest strike I had participated in. There were little strikes before then, if you could call them strikes, which really meant just staying away from work for two or three days. Usually only Filipino workers were involved in these strikes. At the time, you see, it seemed that the Filipinos were always on strike for better wages and conditions. These strikes were short in duration, however, and the Filipinos were always pressured back to work, whether or not their demands were met. There were many Mexican workers coming in from Mexico by that time but they did not join these strikes. The Mexicans were recruited by the growers especially when there was a strike in the fields by Filipinos. The contractors got Mexican labor in the asparagus fields during the big Stockton strike too. There were not many Japanese farmworkers by this time. Most had become small farmers themselves before the war and they were busy trying to build up their farms again after losing a lot of property when they were herded to concentration camps around the U.S. during the war. So as usual, only the Filipinos went on strike in the asparagus fields that year.

I don't remember exactly how long that strike lasted but it went on for quite some time. Fortunato and I joined the picket in car caravans. We also went to the headquarters on El Dorado Street and a nearby hotel for meetings. But as the strike continued, pretty soon Fortunato and I ran out of money and could not pay for our room in the hotel. The union couldn't help us with extra money and many of us were becoming financially desperate. I was desperate because I was still supporting my younger brother Martin through law school in Manila. So, since there was no work in Delano because the grapes were not yet ready to be picked, and in Stockton there was the strike, Alaska was the only place left for us to go to. But first Fortunato and I had to go back to Delano and get the little money I had left at the post office. When we left Stockton many months later the strike was still going on.

After I got my money in Delano, my cousin and I immediately took the bus to Seattle where the cannery workers for Alaska were being dispatched from. When we got there we stayed with our cousin Godoy who was then married to a white woman. Fortunato was dispatched to Alaska almost immediately because he already had seniority since he had worked in the Alaskan canneries before and was already a union member. But I was not yet a union member. There was only one more job opening and it was between me and this other guy who didn't have seniority either. Well, Godoy was able to help me by talking to some union official he knew into giving me the job. He also worked on the business agent who dispatched the workers, pressuring him a bit, I guess. So, instead of the other guy the agent took me and my name was the last on the list that was going to Alaska. I was even accompanied to the pier by a friend who came just to make sure I got on that boat. I was very lucky.

It was springtime, and the trip from Seattle to Alaska took about four days, and the boat stopped at many ports. The cannery we were going to was called the "Alitak," after an Indian village nearby and it was on Kodiak Island. That was my first time in Alaska and the last too, for I never went back after that job.

When I got there I learned that the workers didn't get paid until after the contract was completed and that we would receive our salaries back in Seattle. The native Alaskans complained about this policy because they didn't get any business from the migrant workers who didn't have any money to spend there. Well, I was worried because that meant I couldn't send money to my brother in Manila. So I went to talk to the bookkeeper of the company. I told him why I needed the money, that I was putting my brother through law school, and if I didn't send money he would have to quit school. I said, "I don't have to explain to you the necessity of having money when you're going to school because I'm sure you went to school yourself and that's why you've got this job." He listened and then said, "Well, I can't send your money directly to the Philippines from here but if you know somebody in Seattle who can send it to your brother I can arrange it." He gave me a check for a hundred dollars. I sent it to Godoy's wife and asked her to send it to my brother.

Again, I was very lucky.

My job at the cannery was what was called "filling cans." The process went like this: first, the butchers cut off the fish heads and sent the fish to the fishwash where they were cleaned. Then everything went through a machine which cut them up and canned them. My job was to pull out the underweight cans from one of the conveyor belt lines, fill them up to the required weight, then put them back on the main line that then took the cans through a sealer machine. That was all I did, a repetitious performance that made me dizzy watching all those cans in motion like a flowing stream of water.

At that time the workers in Alaska lived better than their counterparts in Delano because the Alaskan workers were protected by a strong union. The bunkhouse for the workers in Alaska was in good condition, for example, and the food was furnished by the company. We were paid our salary plus room and board. There was a cook, baker, dishwasher, and a couple of waiters even. No doubt those were better conditions than what we had in Delano. But I was there for only two months because that was the duration of my contract. I received $500 for those two months of work which was good money then.

On our way back to Delano we heard that the asparagus strike in Stockton was over, its success limited but nevertheless it had some success, thanks to the honest leadership of Chris and Ernesto. But at that time—and remember it was only right after World War II—it was very difficult to get support for the plight of farmworkers from the general population. The country was busy increasing its production of everything, including agricultural output in California, so the state of the farmworkers was lost among everything else that was happening in the industry. However, the asparagus strike was an important event for Filipino farmworkers in California. Like their brothers who struck and paralyzed the sugarcane fields in Hawaii in the 1920s, the Stockton strike got the Filipino workers together again in large numbers behind a common cause, and this time with the benefit of better organization. However, nearly 20 more years would pass before the Filipinos would show their strength in numbers and unity again, in the grape fields south of Stockton, in Delano.

∼

When we got back to Delano we were immediately picking grapes again. I remember working for the Caric farms this time of which Louis Caric was the boss. He had two sons, Louis, Jr., and Steve, and he also had a daughter. They all still live in Delano, I believe. The sons are all grown-up now. They have their own families, and are still in the grape business. I worked for their father that summer of 1948 through one winter, pruning grapes.

"A matter of survival"

Life for the farmworkers in the San Joaquin Valley progressed according to the season of the different crops. From summer through winter
it was harvesting and pruning the grapevines; in the spring it was asparagus or some other crop, and in between grape harvest time there
was cannery work in Alaska for those who needed the extra money or
simply got bored in the valley with no work. Many, however, stayed
around in the valley during the slack periods, not doing much except
maybe gambling more often.

I never liked to gamble myself, either with cards or betting on fighting cocks. I also never had an interest in spending my money on clothes
or cars. Many Filipino men liked to dress up too much but I tried to
stay in the middle. In the Philippines it was very important how one
dressed. Clothes were definitely a sign of your social class and it was
impossible for a poor Filipino to afford to buy the kind of clothes that
distinguished a person as well-to-do. So, when the poor Filipinos got
here they discovered that their measly salaries still afforded them the
privilege to dress like a rich guy so they dressed that way. But I didn't
want to be flashy. I always felt I could not afford flashy clothes, and besides, I didn't think it was proper. All I wanted was to appear decent.
People could see that I was poor but as long as I was clean that's all that
mattered. Clothes were not that important to me like they were for others. Sure, I like nice clothes, but if I bought all the clothes I wanted I
wouldn't have been able to help my brother and sister. If I had bought
all the cars I wanted, my brother and sister would not have been educated and their kids wouldn't have gone to school either. So what good
would that have been for me? The new clothes would not stay new and
a nice car would be gone by now, too. So I just spent a little on clothes
and for my little education.

I also didn't like to spend my free time just talking and having fun. I
liked people but I also wanted to be alone a lot and when I was alone I

wasn't worried to death. Perhaps I didn't feel lonesome as much as the others because I read a lot and that occupied my mind. During those first years in Delano, while living in the labor camps and working in the fields, reading was my real pleasure. I didn't need much money for such a pastime since I could get most of my books from the public library. I read mostly about politics. I didn't read novels because for me they were too long. I don't have the patience to finish a novel, not even today. The only novel I remember finishing was *The Jungle* by Upton Sinclair, which I thought was very good. I started to write articles and poems after I finished reading that book. My friend Bill Berg from New York gave it to me.

Bill was one of those rare persons I met in the 1950s who did not see the color of people's skins. He could see that I was brown and he was white, but he was not prejudiced. Because of Bill I learned about many other things too. I learned how to talk to Filipinos about the white man to try to wake them up and make them understand all the sides of the race issue. I'd tell them, for example, that white people had also fought for freedom and are also revolutionaries, that the minority in this country cannot fully succeed without the help of all freedom fighters, whatever the color of their skin. I believe that my thinking like this came from my friendship with Bill Berg.

∽

Because I didn't gamble or spend my money on unnecessary luxuries for myself, the little money I earned I was able to save. Whatever little money I earned I put in the bank, but pretty soon I didn't feel good about the bank making money on my money so I took it out to buy property which became my security instead. This was in the early 1950s. Buying land was not common then among Filipinos but I was one of the few who did. For many reasons Filipinos did not invest their money in that way back then. But that was what I wanted to do—I guess really for personal reasons. My family owned land before in the Philippines but had lost it all. I guess why I started buying property near Delano had something to do with that. Actually, after my family had sold all their land, mostly for survival reasons, there was still a small piece of land in Pangasinan province that my family was entitled to get from an inheritance just after the war. My family wrote me about it. There was, however, a question as to who should have it, my uncle or my brother. I advised my brother to give it up to my uncle because I didn't want quarreling in the family. Besides, Martin was already a lawyer by then and I didn't want my uncle to have to hire his own lawyer to fight for it if he thought it was rightfully his and then possibly lose the land in order to pay for lawyer's fees if the case reached the courts. I'd rather see my cousins get that property because they needed it, too, than have the entire family lose it all to some outsider. So my uncle got the land. Because of this and other reasons, I had this desire to own land. Maybe I just wanted to get back something which I felt I had lost through the family. It's a little confusing to me sometimes because owning land and property are in many ways contrary to my political ideology. I had read some Marxist literature then and I thought Marx's ideas about land ownership were good, but I couldn't apply them to my own situation when I wanted to invest money in land. My best rationale was that it was all for my future security. I figured that if ever I had to quit the labor camps or simply didn't want to work for a while I could at least stay at my own place. When it comes to political ideologies I have always thought practical was a better word than radical.

I had finished supporting Martin and my sister Leonor and taking care of their expenses when I bought my own property. But I continued to live in labor camps even after I bought the house and lot in Richgrove so I could continue saving money. The lots are under my name and I don't owe anything on them now. They're mostly empty lots but one has old houses on it which I get a few dollars for rent. The rent I charge is actually very low—$25 a month (in the late 1970s) for a house. Sometimes the people living there don't pay the rent for many months and I'm reluctant to go by and ask them to pay. I probably lose money but that's the way I am. You know I don't even know how many people live on my property. I don't check-up on these things because I feel that it's none of my business, really.

In the late 1950s, I was able to build a new house in front of the old ones and I left the labor camp to live in that house. It's still not completely finished up to now. The floor was never finished because I couldn't make up my mind if I wanted to put carpet over it or not. When the Delano strike started and I got involved, I didn't have the time or money to fix up the house anymore. That's the way it is even today. It's a nice little house with a good stove and a good sink but it's still sort of a mess.

So there I was in the 1950s, for the first time since I had come to America, more or less free from my obligations to my family back in the Philippines. I will never forget what my father said to me before I left home for the U.S. In our dialect he said, "There's nothing left for your brother and sister now. You take it because you need it. Use it but don't forget that you've got to help them later, too." He was referring to the money I used to pay for my passage to America. It came from the sale of my family's last piece of property. In fact, before that, when I needed money for school supplies—I was in high school then—and other school expenses, my father slowly sold whatever small pieces of land we owned. So my father's words weighed heavy on me and that's why I matured early and took my responsibilities very seriously.

My father was very sickly and never had the strength to work his own land. He was always so pale. I think he was anemic and I knew he was often in pain. Since he couldn't work his own land he leased them out. My father wanted me to help on the land and had no interest in sending me to school. He was an uneducated man and it didn't even occur to him that I should go to school. During my father's time, when the Spaniards still controlled the Philippines, poor people had no opportunities to go to school. But when I was a little boy, the Americans had taken over from the Spaniards as colonial rulers and they introduced the public school system.

Education was like the elusive butterfly for the Filipinos and the Americans were giving it away almost for free to anyone who was interested. There was no law then that required parents to send their children to school but it wasn't necessary because almost every family, it

seemed, except mine, wanted to send their children. I was a very determined young boy and begged my parents to send me to school but my
father would just say, "Look at the *carabao* (water buffalo). It doesn't
need school, so why do you?" I waited a whole year for them to change
their mind and when they refused I just went on my own and went to
school. My parents found out about it only later from a relative because
I didn't want to tell them right away. I remember that after the initial
surprise they just laughed when they found out that I had been going to
school all on my own. They never got angry or questioned me about it.
They just accepted it. They always accepted my independent nature but
once I started going to school my father knew that he wouldn't be able
to hold on to the land.

I don't think my father felt bad about having to sell his land to support me through school because I was their only child for 17 years. I had
four brothers who all died very young. My parents also adopted a first
cousin of mine because her mother had died early but that child died
too. Two of my brothers died very young and the other two lived to be
one or two years old. It was very hard on my mother because she was
not a strong woman emotionally. She became hysterical for a long time
after a child died. All these deaths only made her more attached to me. I
was almost 17 years old when Leonor, my sister, was born, and Martin,
the youngest, came along two or three years after Leonor. So you see,
when I left the Philippines in 1926, in my early twenties, my brother
and sister were still babies, and I have not seen them since then.

When I moved out of the labor camps to live in my own house, I was
satisfied that I had helped my brother and sister with their education
and to get started with their careers and had therefore fulfilled my obligations to my family. And even though I didn't have to send money to
Martin anymore by then because he was already an established lawyer, I
sent him some on occasion. Once I sent him about $300. Another time
Martin wrote and said he would like to buy books for his library and I
knew that a law library can cost a lot so I sent him $2,500. Then, he
changed his mind and wrote me that he wanted to do something else
with the money. Then he changed his mind again and said he'll buy the

books after all. He was fluctuating between his new library and building his family a new house. My mother told him, "But you need the house, too." So I wrote him and I said, "I gave you the money because you need it, as long as you don't throw it away, it's good enough for me whatever you want to use it for. Use your own judgment." So he built a house. I suppose he needed the house more than he needed the library.

There were so many things that I had done for my brother that I don't even think he knows about. Oh, I know he's aware of the money I sent him and that he's very appreciative. But there were other little things that I had to help him out with. One particular incident I remember took place when he was in the fourth grade. He had just transferred to a new school from another province and because he was new in class the teacher wasn't paying much attention to him. Our father had just died and Martin wrote me several times explaining that since his transcripts from his previous school had been lost by the school, that this particular teacher wouldn't let him take the examination that would allow him to pass on to the next grade. Martin wrote that our mother was very concerned but didn't know what to do. I felt very proud in my heart that my brother could write me such good letters in English when he was so young about such an important issue. I knew that he wanted to work hard in school so it was important that he not be held back just because of a mix-up with his transcript. I immediately wrote the Director of the Bureau of Education in Manila, Luther B. Buley. I sent him some of the letters Martin had sent me plus his grades, and asked Mr. Buley to investigate why this teacher wouldn't allow Martin to take the final examination because his transcripts were supposedly missing. Mr. Buley looked into the matter and Martin was allowed to take the examination. He passed it and was promoted to the fifth grade. I heard only much later from a cousin that the damn teacher had gone to my mother after this incident and tried to bawl her out because of the pressure that had come down on him from higher ranking school officials.

After Martin finished his studies at the Philippine Law School he worked as an investigator for the Manila Police Department. After that he was appointed judge in Pagadian City, Mindanao, where he and his family still live. When I began living in my own house Martin wrote me, "Come home now. You have helped me and the family, you have worked for half a century." I remember he used the word "century," but I think he meant 25 years. But I didn't want to go home, especially not to retire because I was only 46 years old then. Several years later after their new house was completed my oldest niece wrote me: "Papa has a room for you." So they always prepared for my coming home. In December 1976, Martin again wrote: "I am reiterating my sincere invitation to you to spend the rest of your life here in the Philippines—either in Quezon City with the children, or in Pagadian with me and Ninay. Although you are an American citizen, I still believe that the U.S. is not a good place for old people, but for the young ones who are still strong and can work." But I couldn't explain to my brother then or to anyone why I couldn't go home. Not then or any time, as it turns out.

I never wrote home about my life in the U.S. because, first, I didn't want my mother to get worried about me. If she had known about my hardships here she would have insisted that I come home, but even though life was very hard for me here as a non-white, I felt that my chances of earning enough money to support the family were still much better in the United States than if I were back home.

There was a time, when I returned to Delano after working in Alaska, when Martin wrote me asking if he could come and join me. I didn't want to encourage either my brother or sister to come and live in the U.S. and live as I had. I felt it was much more important for them to finish their education there. I told Martin, "If you want to finish school you had better stay there, schools cost much more here and I will not be able to support you. I don't earn much here but at least each dollar I send you is two pesos there. If you come here you will have to earn your own way. If you want to come you must finish your education first." Well, Martin never came. I might have hurt him or sounded cold when I wrote that. I was trying to be truthful but at the same time I didn't want to tell him the details of how hard life was here. I don't think I wanted a member of my family to come and see for themselves the reality of my life in the States. Now today I wish I had someone here from my immediate family.

I guess there's also a second reason for not writing my family about my hardships: my pride. I couldn't tell them some of the truths about my life here because I wanted to make them believe that America was good as I believed before I left. I had to struggle to make it good, at least for myself. Most of my Filipino compatriots felt this way too, and that's why very few of us wrote truthfully about our lives here to our families back home. Many of us were guilty of fooling our families in the Philippines into believing we were something here that we really were not. I'm afraid, though, that this practice still continues with the more recent Filipino immigrants. When I was with the union, I moved around a lot, talking to different groups and meeting a lot of people, including newly arrived Filipinos. I noticed that many Filipinos coming to this country were just as naive as my group was when we came over 50 years ago. From talking to these Filipinos, I realized they're still not aware of the realities of life in the U.S. Some don't know at all how hard their relatives who came before them had to struggle just to survive. They really don't know what's going on here until they come to see for themselves. Much of this ignorance stems from Filipinos like myself who have been too proud to write home the truth about our existence here.

Like most Filipino pioneers in this country, I became emotionally very sensitive because I, too, was always thinking about going home. I always imagined that even if I did go home I would not live in my brother's house. I wouldn't want to be a bother to anyone because I know that in-laws can sometimes cause trouble. After years of living on my own here, I felt that I would need some sort of independence there. The thought of what I would do there and how I would live was always in the back of my mind. But most of us never went back home for one reason or another. When my mother asked me how long I planned to stay away, I told her three years. Well, I've been here in the U.S. almost 50 years now and I haven't been back yet. That's the way it goes. I didn't plan it that way, I never thought it would happen like this. I thought when I finished school and saved enough money I could go home. But I didn't—I never got through, you see. When I got through with one thing I would never have any money left so I had to go back to work again. I always just had enough money to send home but as far as having enough money for myself to return and lead my own life it never happened. My life here was always just a matter of survival. It was always an emergency and I was never ready to go back. That's the way it has been for most of us Filipino old-timers.

"The most important $2 in my life"

I know I'm not the best person to tell the history of the United Farm Workers. Many books have been written about the union, the farm labor movement, about Cesar Chavez—in fact a lot has been written about Cesar—and the two unions that merged to form the UFW. These were the Agricultural Workers Organizing Committee (AWOC), AFL-CIO, and the National Farm Workers Association (NFWA). A very good book about the UFW is Sam Kushner's *Long Road to Delano*. Kushner was a progressive reporter and he knew the facts about the farmworkers movement better than most.

But I have my own observations about certain aspects of the union's history, too. I've been observing and thinking about the union, the farmworkers movement, and especially the role the Filipinos have played in it, and most of my observations you won't find in the other books. You must realize that as an officer in the UFW, I represented a minority in the union, the Filipinos, and the Filipinos have been used and pulled back and forth by the UFW, the Teamsters, and the growers for many years. But I stayed with the UFW longer than any other Filipino leader because I knew it was basically a good union and I knew that Cesar was doing many good things for the farmworkers. Whatever disillusionment or frustrations I might have felt I just had to put them aside for many years. But since I've resigned from the union I am now able to sit back and reflect on what all my thoughts and experiences in the movement mean, not only for myself but also for my fellow Filipino old-timers as well.

As I tell you my impressions of the farmworkers struggle, I want you to realize something else very important. You see, it's my nature to analyze and criticize. But if I say something against Cesar's way of leading the union, I don't say this to hurt Cesar but only to make a point. I don't criticize individuals but rather the situations. I'll criticize the Filipino as well as the Mexican if I see either one doing something I think is wrong. And you will see that I criticize myself too. I know that misunderstood issues can become destructive and eventually divide individuals and groups, even a union. But I believe workers will unite successfully only when there's better understanding of the issues in their entirety, including honest differences of opinions which could give us a broader view of the solutions to our problems. I especially want to help younger Filipinos to think more critically so they will be better prepared to meet similar challenges than my generation was. In the farmworkers movement, for example, the Filipinos have been hurt simply because they did not clearly understand the issues.

There is no doubt that I could have lived better if I was not in the union. However, what I lost by joining the union were only material things; what I gained were much more important and valuable. I learned about people, about struggling to improve your life along with your fellow workers. I learned new and important things about this country, about economics, about change, and about life. And I received these valuable lessons from my association with the farmworkers movement.

Even though Filipinos have been a visible minority in the U.S. for many years, we've had very few chances to express ourselves politically in our adopted land. One reason is our Filipino nature, our long tradition of seeing issues and events philosophically and not politically. In town plazas back in the Philippines you could always find groups of men arguing over some abstract ideas or questions like, "Does God really exist?" "Can there be true equality among men?" You know, stuff like that. This tradition or nature of Filipinos, coupled with the fact that as "nationals" those of us who came before 1936 could not become U.S. citizens and therefore were not allowed to really participate in any political activity, made it very difficult for Filipinos to organize as a political force. For many years we had to be content with addressing issues on an abstract level rather than questioning the realities that underlined our present conditions. For me it was a real drawback because I was always reading about politics and thinking about national and international issues but what I read I could not apply to my community. Also, it wasn't uncommon to find Filipinos who dabbled in community politics who were just racketeers. It's too bad but that's the way it was.

When the UFW came along it really changed my life. It gave me the opportunity to bring my basically philosophical and questioning nature down to earth, and apply it to real everyday issues that actually affect people's lives. As a Filipino it gave me the opportunity to participate in the political struggles of this country, not as a racketeer as many Filipino community leaders had been, but as a worker struggling along with my fellow workers for our constitutional rights.

The farmworkers movement was only progressing slowly after World War II until the Delano strike in 1965 made it a very popular movement. Throughout the 1950s many Mexicans and Filipinos had been involved with one union or another or some kind of community organization. There were many different activities going on then but all our activities here and there just had not yet come together.

In the late 1950s I belonged to the National Farm Labor Union (NFLU), AFL-CIO. In fact, for a while I was the president of our local here in Delano. This union came before AWOC. Our membership was mostly Filipino, with a few Mexicans and some Blacks too. Although we weren't very strong then our meetings always had a good turnout. Several hundred Filipinos showed up at these meetings; you could see there was always the potential in numbers but it simply hadn't been tapped. And I guess the people at the head of the AFL-CIO realized this also because in 1959 they established AWOC. They could see that the farmworkers movement wasn't getting anywhere and needed some assistance. But AWOC was not a union. It was a branch of the AFL-CIO that did just what its name said—it organized the workers. It was established to get out in the San Joaquin Valley and see if it could get things moving for the AFL-CIO. The director of AWOC was always an Anglo who was sent out to California from back East. Larry Itliong, a Filipino, was hired as one of the first AWOC organizers because AWOC, like the NFLU, was comprised mostly of Filipinos. However, one of the original organizers hired along with Larry was a Mexican, Dolores Huerta. In fact, Dolores told me once she was the one who got Larry into AWOC.

Later, Dolores left AWOC and went to work for Cesar Chavez when he organized the National Farm Workers Association. Since AWOC was Filipino it was only natural for Dolores to feel more comfortable working with Cesar and her own people, the Mexican farmworkers, in the NFWA.

It's kind of a funny story about how I got involved with AWOC. It happened in the mid-1960s and I was already living in my small house in Richgrove. The neighboring property was owned by another Filipino who was already a member of AWOC. His cousin, Ben Gines, was one of the AWOC organizers. Well, one day when I was outside watering the plants, you know, my neighbor asked me from his yard, "Are you a member of the union now?" And I said, "What union?" That's the way it was. Even though I had been involved in the NFLU and was even the president for a while, I had sort of dropped out of things and didn't keep up on every new union or workers' organization. There were so many, you see. Then my neighbor told me about AWOC and I said, "No, I didn't know about it." "Well," he said, "don't you want to be a member?" and I said, "How much is the membership?" "Two dollars." Well, you can see where my interest was then. More on my pocketbook than on politics. In those days I usually had some money in my pocket. I would even carry $100 or so. I had always been frugal with money and by this time I was able to save a little of my small earnings for myself for the first time in my life. So $2 didn't mean much to me and so I gave that amount to my neighbor for membership to AWOC. He said he'd get me a union book. That was just before the big strike in 1965 here in Delano when I started paying my union dues. Actually, I didn't know that the strike had begun until this one guy, Emilio Dasio, didn't come to work on a Monday. I heard some guys asking him, "How come you were off Sunday and then Monday you didn't come to work again?" Emilio said, "The trouble with you guys is that you sign up for something but then you don't do what it says." He was talking about AWOC, as it turns out. "So?" we responded. "They started a strike," Emilio said. "But because you guys are still working and don't want to join the strike how can it succeed? That's why I've decided to come back to work myself. It's useless." But that was only the second day of the AWOC strike. We were working at Jack Radovich's Labor Camp No. 2 in Richgrove. I said to the other guys, "It's no good. Other Filipinos are on strike and we have to help them." So the next day, the third day of the strike I didn't go to work. I went to town instead and looked for the AWOC office but I couldn't find it. I was wandering around, looking for that damn place when someone told me that the office was somewhere around the Takaki Drugstore. So I went there but I still didn't see anybody. There was no office around there. Then someone told me that there were some Filipinos gathered at the Filipino Community Center over on Glenwood Street, so I went there. But the people there were preparing for some kind of beauty contest. Filipinos were always preparing for a beauty queen contest in those days, a favorite pastime along with cockfighting. Anyway, the people there told me to come back in the evening because there was going to be a meeting. I attended that meeting and that was the start of my career with the farmworkers movement and later on, with the UFW which became the most important part of my life. It became my way of life, as a matter of fact. The $2 I paid for membership was probably the most important and expensive $2 I ever spent in my life. I didn't need anyone to convince me then or now that it was the right decision to make. I knew the union was good for the workers. The only thing I didn't know back then was how difficult the struggle would get.

On September 8, 1965, at the Filipino Hall at 1457 Glenwood Street in Delano, the Filipino members of AWOC held a mass meeting to discuss and decide whether to go on strike or accept the reduced wages proposed by the growers. The decision was "to strike" and it became one of the most significant and famous decisions ever made in the entire history of the farmworkers labor struggles in California. It was like an incendiary bomb, exploding out the strike message to the workers in the vineyards, telling them to have sit-ins in the labor camps, and set up picket lines at every grower's ranch. There had been small strikes in Delano before but this was the first major strike. The strikes before that one would last only two or three days. But this one, started solely by

Filipinos, took five years. It was the strike that eventually made the UFW, the farmworkers movement, and Cesar Chavez famous worldwide and it lasted until 1970 when we finally won our workers' contracts with the growers.

～

To understand the history of the Delano grape strike, you must also understand the geography and weather of California. The first season for picking grapes starts in the hottest part of the state, in the south in places like Coachella. When the workers finish picking grapes there, the work starts moving up north as the grapes ripen with warmer weather in the grape-growing regions of Arvin-Lamont and finally, Delano. The grape-picking season, therefore, moves from south to north.

The Delano strike really started in the south and then spread all the way up to Delano. In Coachella at the start of the season, the AWOC Filipinos demanded a wage of $1.40 an hour. The growers decided quickly to pay the price because if the workers left the fields there would be no one to pick the grapes for, unlike the northern grape areas like Delano, there were few resident workers around Coachella, and having to wait for substitute workers would be economically unfeasible for the growers. You see, with the early grape harvest season in Coachella the growers could get the highest prices for their grapes. They sold for $10 to $14 a lug—which is 28 pounds—and sometimes the price they asked was even higher than that. The way they saw it, they'd rather give that lousy extra dime raise to the workers and get the early high profits from the grapes. Here in Delano there's a steady work force because the workers live in the area while in Coachella the workers would come from Delano and other areas, even from Mexico and Texas. If there is a strike in Coachella, the workers would simply leave and go home, and the few local residents couldn't pick all the grapes, so the grapes would be left to rot and the growers would lose their profits.

From Coachella the workers moved north, from Arvin-Lamont and then to Delano. Most of the workers from Coachella live in the Delano area, so when they got to Delano for the grape harvest they naturally expected the same wages: $1.40 an hour. But they were wrong. The growers in Delano didn't want to pay that kind of money. With the grape season well underway, the growers knew that by the time the Delano grapes were ready for harvesting, they wouldn't be able to get as much money for their grapes on the market compared to the early part of the season. Since their profits would be a little less, they tried to minimize their profit loss by paying the workers less.

So you see? It's always the same old thing: the profits of the growers versus the wages of the workers. And anybody can see who gets the bad end of the deal. It's always the workers who suffer, never the grower. Just compare the way the two groups live, for example. The growers have their big houses with swimming pools and air conditioners, and cars with air conditioning, all paid for by keeping the workers' wages low. And look at the way the farmworkers live, especially the Filipinos. They live in labor camps. They don't have telephones, no air-conditioning, no heater in winter except maybe for a stove. The toilets, kitchen, and showers are open to the outside. It's hell and they have lived that way everyday of their lives here in this country. And why? So the growers can make bigger and bigger profits and expand their businesses. This is not a new situation. Filipinos in Delano have worked in the grape vineyards for a long time, and back in the Depression years when times were hard for everyone, they were even harder for the Filipino grape pickers. Old-timers have told me about the common practice of hiring during those years. They said that in the pruning season a grower required that new employees report at the labor camp for two, three, or more days and work without pay as trainees. During this training period the farmworker had to pay 75 cents a day for board to the grower. At least the Black slaves in the South had their meals for free. But those Filipino "trainees" paid for their own meals on top of board while working in the farms without pay. Then after the new recruits "learned" the job—although mind you, most Filipino farmworkers had done only this kind of work since they came to this country, oh, some for 20 years—they were paid 10 cents or 15 cents an hour.

During the Great Depression when jobs were scarce, Filipinos were often blamed for taking away jobs from whites. Racist growers and politicians picked on Filipinos as easy targets for discrimination and attack. Filipinos were harassed and driven from their camps and usually wouldn't have anywhere to go. They were pushed to the wall and the whole town was often against them. The police would make false arrests and throw them in jail and then in certain cases the courts imposed excessive fines. Those poor, unfortunate Filipinos risked their lives just to go and buy their groceries. There were bad race riots in the labor camps. Filipinos were hurt and one was even shot dead in bed.[2]

Of course the extra profits that growers make at the expense of the farmworkers are also paid for by the people in the cities who pay higher prices for the goods in the markets. You know, the growers try to fool the consumer by telling them the reason they must pay high prices for their food is because those damn farmworkers want to get paid too high. Well, that's bullshit. The price of food is high because the growers, and mainly the huge agribusinesses and their distributors, are taking such big profits.

When I was working in the fields, I remember that it wasn't beyond some growers to increase their profits by selling premature grapes. The workers with many years experience knew the grapes, and with the first picking of the seedless Thompson grapes, they often complained that the bunches were still too green for picking. It sort of bothered their conscience to pick grapes that weren't yet ready. But the growers gave the orders to pick and pack anyway because the price in the market was high. After the day's picking and packing the state inspector would come to the packing house and inspect the grapes. If he found the contents deficient in quality he would tell the owners to stop the picking. Then the whole crew would be ordered to repack the green grapes—leaving out those that were not yet ready—without pay. While the workers were busy repacking, the inspector watched closely. But when he left, the grower would tell the workers to load the sour grapes first into the boxcar with the repacked boxes on top. This was one of the magic tricks of the growers in the table-grape industry. Along with brands from other ranches the Delano "sour grapes" were sent as delicacies to cities all over the United States. The uniform bunches and solid berries, packed beautifully, could have been the choice grapes of the world if the growers only waited just a few more days for nature to sweeten the fruit.

Premature harvest in the grape industry has been the common practice of both the family farm and large agribusiness. It is caused by cutthroat competition tainted with deceit and unsatisfied personal greed. Customers spend their money for sour grapes not fit to eat. The orders from the growers overpower the conscience and decency of workers to do what is right in their work. Agribusinesses sell food all over the world—to Latin America, India, Asia, and Russia. The price of food continues to go up but the workers continue to remain poor. The agribusiness is the single largest industry in the U.S., and it is big and successful only because of the farmworkers. Yet, the farmworkers do not receive any of the wealth generated by their own labor. The American agribusiness industry has been developed mainly by the labor, sweat, and blood of imported minorities. It has been subsidized by cheap wages, miserable housing conditions and the lives of pioneering labor leaders. You see, the issue is always the same: agribusiness wants to control the workers. They don't want the situation to be reversed. Control and exploitation of the workers through low wages and of the consumers through high prices keep agribusiness going.

∽

Although AWOC won a victory in Coachella, it should only be considered in retrospect a half-victory. We won the salary increase but we didn't get a contract, and in a labor negotiation, the salary is really secondary to a contract. If you don't get a contract it means the growers have not recognized your union. It was a very big mistake on the part of the AWOC leadership to give up the fight without getting a contract. Al Green was the AWOC director then and was responsible for the decisions. Although there were Filipino organizers like Larry Itliong, Ben Gines, and Pete Manuel, the final decisions were made by the director.

There were many questionable decisions made by the AWOC directors. Norman Smith was the first AWOC director and he started out by recruiting winos and bums on skid row instead of real farmworkers. Naturally he was not successful because these kind of guys were not reliable. When Al Green took over the directorship, he signed contracts with labor contractors and not with the growers directly. That was also a mistake. We all knew that the labor contractors also exploited workers and since they were really just employees of the growers if you didn't go after the growers you were just wasting your time.

There were times when we saw the AWOC director hanging around with and seeming to be quite friendly with the Teamsters organizers. Everyone knew that the AWOC director worked for the AFL-CIO and that the AFL-CIO and the Teamsters were in direct competition, both vying for the membership of the Filipinos. This really confused the AWOC Filipinos and it was this manner of handling their business and some of the kinds of decisions being made by the AWOC directors that one can question.

The problem was that the decision-making in AWOC was made only at the top by white directors who were not farmworkers themselves, when the strength of the organization came from the bottom, from the Filipino membership. I think the unity and strength of the Filipinos in AWOC, and for years to follow, in the UFW, was greatly damaged by the poor decisions made by the leadership of AWOC which came from the AFL-CIO. Maybe these mistakes were unintentional—I don't know—but those guys who came from the AFL-CIO were union professionals, they weren't farmworkers or Filipinos and they didn't understand the subtleties of our situation as farmworkers in California.

When the Filipino farmworkers went on strike in Delano on September 8, 1965, they made that decision on their own without the explicit support of the AWOC director and the AFL-CIO leadership. That decision, as it turned out, was an extremely important one, because it started the ball rolling for the great farmworkers movement of the 1960s that soon thereafter led to the historic formation of the United Farm Workers, the UFW under the charismatic leadership of Cesar Chavez. What the Filipinos knew at the time was that this strike would paralyze the growers and it did. The Filipinos in 1965 had to be united in order to pull the strike off. We had a strong labor consciousness. We had been working in this country for over 40 years, and we were aware of prices and profits because we listened to market reports on the radio and then discussed these reports in Ilocano, our dialect. This "workers' conscious-ness" helped us to be the most organized and united of all the different ethnic groups of farmworkers at that time. Most of the Mexican work-ers were new arrivals and because of their large numbers and diversity of movement they were not yet as well-organized as the Filipinos, al-though Chavez was then working with his people on that. When times got bad the Mexicans could still just pick-up and go back to Mexico. But not the Filipino.

For many of the growers the Filipino was his primary worker, actu-ally favoring the Filipino worker over any other worker for several rea-sons. For one thing, the greater numbers of Filipino workers were single men. Most were recruited as young men in the Philippines, and the anti-miscegenation laws that existed in the U.S. for many years made it difficult for them to raise families. As a single male, the Filipino was very cheap to house. Often the grower would even pay the Filipino a little bit more than the Mexican or some other worker because the Fili-pino had stayed in the area for many years and he knew the work. There are many skills to be learned in working in the fields, and the growers knew the Filipino was already a very experienced worker who required no extra training. So the growers found the Filipino worker to be very convenient: he was single, he was experienced, he was cheap to main-tain, and he was always available. To the grower, this was important, because it meant higher profits for him. This created, however, a unique predicament for the Filipino. He was a prized worker for the grower but at the same time he was ready to be organized and to struggle for his rights. Because of their unique situation the Filipinos were torn be-tween the growers, the Teamsters, and the UFW.

Being split into different factions by the competing groups for their loyalty and service, the Filipinos, already a minority in numbers among farmworkers in California at that time—you could say they were a mi-nority within a minority—became an easily manipulable element within the farmworkers movement. Everyone wanted to control the farm-workers and especially the Filipinos—the growers so that they could control their own profits; the UFW in order to build its base so it could struggle against the more powerful growers and other competing unions, especially the Teamsters; and the Teamsters out of competition with the AFL-CIO. Unions often fought over representation of the workers because there was a lot of money involved in workers' pension plans. Too often big unions like the Teamsters forgot about the workers and became too interested in the power generated by these huge pension plans.

At the same time that the Filipinos in AWOC were fighting for their rights as workers, Cesar Chavez and many Mexicans were doing the same thing through the NFWA. Sometimes AWOC and NFWA would cooperate in a strike or some activity, but most of the time we were just acting alone. Before Cesar got involved with the NFWA, he was with the CSO—the Community Service Organization. Fred Ross, Sr., was the person responsible for CSO which was not backed by a union but some kind of a foundation headed by Saul Alinsky from Chicago. Alinsky was a sociologist who understood the worker's psychology and applied his knowledge and ideas to stir people up. He called himself a rebel but I think he was more of a reformer than a revolutionary. He believed in American capitalism but he also wanted to stir up issues and awaken the sleeping uneducated workers to get up and organize and fight for their own welfare. I know that Alinsky's strength was that he was a good strategist of movement dynamics. Cesar learned a lot from working under the influence of Alinsky's ideas which he got from his direct apprenticeship with Fred Ross, Sr. I don't think enough credit has been given to Fred because it was he, more than any other person, who had the biggest influence on Cesar's way of thinking and ideas. Cesar didn't develop on his own. Cesar had very little education and not much preparation as a community organizer. It was Fred's tutorship and guidance in the ways of the movement and union management that more than anything else turned Cesar from a zoot suit leader in the *Sal, si puedes* streets to the director of the most famous farmworkers movement in the world.

I have known Fred Ross since 1965 and I have heard a lot about his close relationship with Cesar and how Cesar was being prepared as a leader in the CSO and then later on, the NFWA. I was impressed when I first met Fred because he showed he had a lot of patience, persistence, and desire to help organize the poor working people like the Mexicans in California. The growers used to spread around propaganda that Fred Ross and Cesar Chavez and some others were students of Alinsky. The propaganda made it seem like they were actually in a special school run by Alinsky in Chicago. It's kind of funny because the growers saw Alinsky as some kind of a radical revolutionary, but as I said, he really wasn't all that radical. But the growers were afraid of him and they wanted to make it look as if Chavez, Ross, and the others working with them were special agents of Alinsky. This wasn't true at all. Fred never went to any school of Alinsky's. After Fred finished college he got a job with the State of California as an organizer in one of the state-funded agencies. Fred learned about organizing on his own because of this job, not from some training program run by Alinsky. Alinsky had gotten some money and formed a foundation to help poor people. In the 1960s he became interested in expanding his operations to California. He was looking for good organizers and had heard about Fred. At first Alinsky wanted Fred to organize Black workers. But Fred told Alinsky that he would rather organize the Mexicans since that's what he had been doing already. I don't think Alinsky really knew what was going on out here in California. He was back in Chicago and there the dominant minority workers are Blacks. But Fred knew that in California the Mexican workers were growing in number, and that when organized, had the potential to make a strong movement.

Since the UFW was established, Fred's job continued to be that of a teacher in organizing. He was in charge of the union's educational department. Fred is really an educator who has learned through his own practical experience what he knows about organizing. He didn't study it in books. For example, Fred was the originator of the "house meeting" idea which the UFW has used to great success and which originally led to the formation of the CSO. Unfortunately, middle-class Mexican-

Americans started using the CSO for their own economic and political expedience and killed its original intent. However, the CSO spirit and ideal were resurrected by Fred and Cesar in the new service organization, the NFWA.

The idea behind the house meeting was to gather a small group to discuss a pertinent issue in one of the worker's homes. Then when there was a big enough group a bigger meeting would be called, this time a mass meeting. This concept worked well because when the issues are very controversial and you are dealing with workers who are not sophisticated in the ways of labor unions, politics, and the like, you have to first earn their trust by talking with them in their own houses. You cannot organize them if you just talk to them on the streets. You've got to be friendly. Then you can get them to participate and not be suspicious about you or your abilities or intentions. So that was the process. It's the kind of organizing that takes a lot of footwork, and especially patience. To go and sit and talk to people in their houses you have to really care for the people. Fred and Cesar are that way and I think that's why it worked so well. It was a logical system of organizing and to this day it is still being used by the UFW. For that idea and many others credit should go to Fred Ross, Sr.

Six months after the Delano strike started, the NFWA organized the historic farmworkers march from Delano to Sacramento in March 1966 to demonstrate the issue further than the picket lines. This was a new sensation for the people. Hundreds joined in and thousands of people gathered in front of the Capitol. This march certainly put the Delano grape strike into the national spotlight. Farmworkers and sympathizers became aware of the struggle and began trickling, and later pouring, into the movement. Some of us in AWOC also joined the march, although against the wishes of our director then, Al Green. Some went halfway, some went all the way to Sacramento, a 200-mile trek. This march scared the Schenley Industries in particular, a big landowner in Delano. They were afraid of a boycott of their products. So while the people were still on the march, the Schenley people called up and wanted to talk to Cesar and said that they were willing to negotiate with the farmworkers. Everybody was really excited upon hearing that.

It was after that march when the AFL-CIO recognized the strength of a merger between AWOC and NFWA and strongly encouraged it. But for both unions to merge into one strong union was not easy. There were many problems to be overcome. First, there was the Teamsters to contend with because they had also been trying to organize farmworkers, primarily citrus workers. For AWOC there were more problems with the Teamsters, because although AWOC was an AFL-CIO project, AWOC director Al Green was very close to the Teamsters organizer in the area, Jim Smith. I think they were personal friends. Al was also encouraging the Teamsters to get involved in organizing the farmworkers. I even heard that in Lindsay, California, the Teamsters and AWOC shared the same office. Their funds were getting mixed up, which was not proper, but also presented added problems to the question of a merger between AWOC and NFWA.

So understandably, the Teamsters used a lot of propaganda to keep the Filipinos from agreeing to a merger between AWOC and the NFWA under the national union umbrella of the AFL-CIO. They wanted AWOC to secede from the AFL-CIO and join the Teamsters instead. When we started the grape strike here in Delano right away, Teamsters organizer Jim Smith came to the Filipino Hall to talk to us. He told us that the Teamsters were the biggest union in the whole country, more than 2.2 million members then. Well, that impressed some of our people. He said it was the richest union and had lots of political power. It also controlled the trucking industry and therefore it would be more logical for the farmworkers to align themselves with the Teamsters instead of the AFL-CIO. I remember Jim Smith saying to us, "The AFL-CIO isn't doing anything."

The Teamsters also tried to scare the Filipinos by telling them that since there were many more Mexican workers than Filipinos, that the Mexicans would soon take over their jobs. Some Filipinos believed this and spoke out against the merger. They feared that merging with the larger Mexican group would leave the Filipinos without power and they would be left with nothing. They reacted that way out of a feeling of self-preservation and protection. All this Teamsters propaganda sounded very convincing to some Filipinos and it caused a real split among AWOC members. This problem of the Filipinos being divided between the Teamsters and the AFL-CIO had been a continual thorn in the side of the farmworkers movement. Those of us in AWOC who favored the merger argued that we must unite all the races so we'll have one strong union that represents all workers. We explained how in the past you could see that because the workers were divided they were weak.

In my own way of reasoning about labor unions, I think the most important thing is getting people together. The farmworkers unions in the past were ineffective because they were factional. You had Filipinos alone, and Mexicans alone, and whites alone. Then the non-whites scab on the others and vice-versa. If you study labor movements you find out that the workers always suffer when they are split into different factions. The owners of the companies, in our case the growers, like to have the workers split so they can play one group of workers off against the others and maximize their own profits and control over the industry. There's nothing new about this. It goes back to the start of the agricultural industry in California.[3]

I realized that there would be problems in merging groups that represented different ethnic groups, but I felt we could never hope to get anywhere unless we merged. Divided we would always be defeated by the growers. Whatever problems that would come about because of the merger we would have to deal with but I felt those problems would be minor compared to the advantages we would gain through our unity. When I was working on the farms I'd go to the library and check out books about labor movements and these books gave me new ideas. I learned something from reading about the "Wobblies," the Industrial Workers of the World. They were the ones who first experimented with the idea of one big labor organization in the whole country. They saw the potential of a national, and even an international, organization of workers and I think that way too.

On the other side, the NFWA membership was also going through difficulties in deciding about the merger. Their members were also kind of split. Some didn't want to merge because they knew that the Filipinos were the favored workers of the growers and many of the foremen were Filipinos. The Mexicans also saw how much better organized the Filipinos were at that time and some felt that they could be controlled by the Filipinos if there was a merger. So you see, both Filipinos and Mexicans suffered from the same fears, insecurities, and prejudices.

Then Bill Kircher was sent by AFL-CIO leader George Meany to talk to both organizations and to encourage their members to merge. Bill was the Director of Organization for the AFL-CIO. He acted as the conduit between the Mexicans and the Filipinos.

Both groups realized the seriousness of the decision and the members of both organizations discussed it a lot. With two separate groups in the strike, things were getting disorganized. AWOC didn't know what NFWA was doing and vice-versa. Incidents that took place on the picket lines were often relayed like rumors, and since we would hear different versions of the same event, we just assumed that very little information was truly reliable. After talking with Bill Kircher, Cesar understood the urgency of the situation and accepted the idea of the merger.

Kircher continued to push hard for a merger because it was becoming obvious that our opponents were far more numerous than just the Teamsters. The State and National Farm Bureau Association, plus a legion of ultra-conservative supporters such as the National Labor Contractors Association and many others, backed-up the rich, local Growers Club in their fight against our strike. Their political spokesmen and defenders ranged from Delano city contractor and councilman Frank Herrera to Richard Nixon, who was then on his way to the White House. The most outspoken demagogues, aside from the obscure councilman from Delano and the future president of the United States, were State Senator John Harmer and U.S. Senator George Murphy.

AWOC's Al Green and Larry Itliong finally went to talk to Cesar Chavez before the merger. Al did not want the merger to happen because I think he was afraid of Cesar. He just wanted to protect his own position. As for Larry Itliong, who was the most powerful Filipino labor leader within AWOC—already a noted labor leader among his people—at first, he too was against the merger. He believed that the Filipinos would be completely dominated by the Mexicans by sheer numbers if the two organizations merged. However, after talking with Cesar, he started to see the benefits of the other side of the argument, the chance for the first time of building one strong farmworkers union. Larry remained skeptical about the merger but he kept his feelings to himself. His primary goal was to improve the working conditions of all farmworkers, although he feared this would be done at the expense of the Filipinos. If Larry had come out publicly against the merger it would never have been as successful as it was nor would Cesar Chavez have been able to rise to the prominent position he now holds in labor history. Larry and the Filipinos held that much power then. So, the way Larry showed his support for the merger was actually by not opposing it. It's ironic that probably the most important thing Larry ever did to help the UFW was just keeping his mouth shut and not voicing some of his deepest feelings, and thereby giving his indirect support to the merger. Very few people even today understand how difficult a decision that was for Larry. He made a tremendous sacrifice. However, after several years in the UFW, Larry quit because he could no longer reconcile his differences with Cesar and some of the advisors and members of the executive board.

It was in August 1966, a year after the Delano strike started, when AWOC and NFWA merged and became the United Farm Workers Organizing Committee, or the UFWOC, AFL-CIO. This merger was supported by the vast majority of Filipino and Mexican farmworkers.

It's really difficult to say how many members AWOC had before the merger because many of those who were on strike were not bonafide members since they were not paying dues. Some people claim the NFWA was a larger group before the merger but I doubt it. Of course they had a much larger potential membership because there were far more Mexican laborers in California than Filipinos. The growers, in the early 1960s, through the Bracero Program, were bringing in thousands of new Mexican laborers to work at wages far below what the Filipinos and Mexicans already in California were getting. After the Bracero Program ended in 1964, many of the braceros returned to the U.S. without proper papers and joined the continually growing Mexican work force.

It's true, though, that in the process of the merger some Filipinos left the AFL-CIO. Ben Gines was one of the Filipino leaders who went over to the Teamsters instead of joining with Chavez's group. That was an honest decision he had to make for himself at the time. After a while with the Teamsters, he quit but never did anything to hurt the other Filipinos' efforts in the UFW. I have a lot of respect for Ben for making that kind of a decision and acting the way he did. Ben had another trade, too, besides being a farmworker and labor organizer. He repaired watches and after he quit the Teamsters, he didn't want to go back to the farms and was able to support his family that way.

At the time of the merger, I counted about seven other Filipinos who went with Ben over to the Teamsters. Of course, it was only a very small part of the Filipino striking force but it was like the tip of an iceberg. You see, later on when the UFW made mistakes in the Hiring Hall about dispatching jobs, and some Filipinos felt they weren't being treated fairly, many of them switched over to the Teamsters. Whatever real or unreal problems existed between the Mexicans and the Filipinos in the UFW, the Teamsters and the growers were always there to fan the flames.

∾

Most of the officers of the NFWA were kept intact and became officers of the new UFW. From the Filipino leaders of AWOC they got Larry Itliong, Andy Imutan, and me. A compromise was worked out between the Mexicans and the Filipinos so that Cesar became director and Larry was assistant director. The UFW was for many years more of an ad hoc organization because we weren't able to have our first official convention and elect officers until 1971. So in the meantime some of us were called vice-presidents, but that term was really confusing because we had a director and an assistant director but no president. Dolores Huerta once said, "Well, so who am I now?" She got confused since she was the secretary before in the old NFWA when Cesar was president. So Cesar said to her, "You are a vice-president now."

When we were introduced by Cesar or other people, for courtesy's sake, you know, because we didn't have official titles yet and since we were supposed to be on the board of directors, we were called vice-presidents of the union. And of course this included me because I had been in the leadership of AWOC. When people came around, Cesar and other union members would say, "This is Philip Vera Cruz, one of the vice-presidents of the union." And some visitors sometimes asked, "How many vice-presidents do you have?"

At that time I went around to speak to people coming to the Filipino Hall to hear about the new union. This was during the time that we had these big caravans to bring food, clothing, money, and people together, and inform them about the UFW. The hall was full then and we used to have big crowds there. Well, someone would ask me, "Who are you?" and I would have to answer, "I'm one of the vice-presidents," because that's what Cesar was saying. But once or twice I was put on the spot because someone asked, "Were you elected?" And I had to tell a lie because it really didn't sound right if you said that you were not elected by the people. Then some people wanted to know how we got our positions, see? Sometimes I just said that since we didn't really have a formal union yet because we were an organizing committee, that we were just steering the operations until there would be an election.

By the time the union finally had its first election of officers in 1971, Pete Velasco and I were the only Filipinos left in the leadership circle. All the others—Larry, Andy, and the rest—had already quit because of disagreements and differences with Cesar. I was elected second vice-president mainly because I was supported by the other board members. Cesar, of course, was elected president and Dolores Huerta first vice-president. There were other Filipinos who were also nominated to be officers and who had support from certain areas, a regional kind of backing from the area where they came from. But anyway, if you didn't have the backing of Cesar and the other board members you couldn't get elected. In the UFW the members just follow the recommendations of the leaders and primarily of Cesar. So I really don't know if I was the popular choice of the Filipino farmworkers or not. In fact, many of the Filipinos didn't even vote in the elections. All I know is that I was the choice of Cesar and the board. This situation was actually detrimental to my effectiveness as a leader because when I differed with Cesar over an issue I couldn't take my case to the union members. It was as if I held my office simply because Cesar approved of me and not the union members necessarily. Larry used to complain that the Filipinos didn't support their leaders enough, and consequently, the Filipino leaders had no real power within the union and I think he was correct in this observation. How could a Filipino with no support from his own people go to Cesar and say this and that and expect to impress upon Cesar that he should be listened to?

"So close to the good life"

When I think of all my experiences in the U.S. since I landed in Washington in 1926, I can't help but think that all of my adult life I've been involved in labor issues. Like most of my compatriots who came on the same boat with me, and even those who came ten or twenty years before us, I've worked in all sorts of jobs that took me across the country.

I came to America on my own and not as a recruited worker as many Filipino men at the time. I came because I had heard good things about the country, especially from the American teachers I had in high school in the provinces. The idea of going to America actually came to me while I was a high school student in Lingayen. I had a German-American teacher who was from Montana—Ida Martner was her name—a very nice lady who talked a lot about the opportunities for young people in the U.S. When I told her I thought all Americans were rich, she told me that wasn't true; that there were many poor students in the U.S. who worked their way through school. But anyone who was willing to work hard could make it in America. That really sounded good to me. Of course she didn't talk about racism in America but then, maybe because she came from Montana, she wasn't as aware of the racial problem since Montana was a sparsely populated state then. I'd go home from her class pretty excited about the idea of going to America. When I told my mother about my idea she said, "But you don't know anybody there." I told her that the Americans were good people and she replied, "Yes, but they don't know you." In the Philippines, you see, when you moved you always moved to a place where you knew someone. So my mother couldn't understand that anyone would want to go to a place without friends or relatives living there. I didn't understand this myself back then, but this didn't stop me from dreaming about going to America anyway. Little did my mother or I know that I was to meet a lot of cousins and relatives when I reached the mainland U.S.

In the early 1920s, people back home were always talking about going to America, to Hawaii in particular. So there was this general excitement. I guess it's not so different for Filipinos in the Philippines today. Many still dream of coming to the U.S. But, back then, America was the "land of opportunity," no doubt about it. We heard friends tell stories from letters they received from relatives in the U.S. telling them how much they were earning, and photographs of these people abroad were always passed around. When I was in grade school, my aunt Leona talked about the letters she got from her stepson, Fabian Romero, who was in California then. I remember one success story in particular because it was about a guy who had the same name as my future sister-in-law, Gorospe. He returned to the Philippines after living in America for several years. He returned with an American accent and got a job as a supervising teacher right away. Later on I heard he was working in Manila and was getting paid four pesos a day. At that time a policeman got 12 pesos a month, which was considered a good wage. But this guy was making four pesos a day! Hell, I didn't even know what he was doing but I was impressed. Then we heard he even bought a big house for his family.

It was success stories like these, plus the impression made upon us by American teachers, that inspired many young Filipino men to go to America. All the stories we heard were only success stories. So my plan was to finish college in America, get a good job over there, save my money, and then return home and support my family. It was only after I finally got to America that I understood how different reality was for us Filipinos living here from the stories we heard back home. As it turned out, it wasn't as simple as I thought. I worked, went to school when I could, then dropped out of school completely before getting a college degree because I had to work full-time to make ends meet. And that's the way it continued for me ever since.

I planned to go to America with Pedro de la Cruz who was a second cousin of my father. He lived in Lapog and I was then living in Asingan, far to the south. It's funny because we never discussed when or where we would meet. He just said when he was ready to leave he'd come to Asingan and get me. So I dropped out of high school on my third year and just waited for Pedro. I knew if I stayed in high school any longer I wouldn't have enough money left to pay for the passage. Several weeks passed and I waited and wondered if Pedro would come or not. Then one night I heard my name being called outside the house. I looked out the window and saw Pedro. He finally arrived and the next day we visited some relatives in a nearby barrio where we were told there were two other young men who were also planning to go to America. We got acquainted with them and someone said, "If you're going and we're also going, why don't we all go together?" Just like that, four of us made our plans—Pedro and me, Gervacio Gorospe, the youngest among us, and Felipe Argel, the oldest. Many years later I heard that Gervacio had died in Tacoma, Washington. The story I heard was that he met and fell in love with a white girl. But it didn't work out between them and he killed himself.

A few days after the four of us got together for the first time, we met again in Asingan and from there we took the bus to Dagupan and then caught the train to Manila. In Asingan I said goodbye to my family. They knew I was leaving. My mother had been crying for over a week already. She really touched me, I loved her very much. But the pull to go away was much stronger. She was really crying that day when we left. My father, who never cried before, was crying too. That was the first and last time I saw him cry. I never could have imagined it then but that would also be the last time I was ever to see them all again. I don't cry much just like my father, but there are certain things that touch me, and that day I was also crying. It's something I don't think about often but that day, leaving my family, it's the only thing that still makes me cry. The whole family watched as we got on the bus as it stopped to pick us up on the road close to our house. It was hard because it was I who was leaving.

When we got to Manila we stayed in the apartment of Felipe's girlfriend, Rita. She lived there with her brother. This was the first time for all of us to be in Manila, our first big city so we were eager to look around. We walked and walked until we came to a very wide street. It was a two-way road and the traffic was very heavy. We wanted to cross but were afraid because of the cars. So we just kept walking against the traffic. We saw a policeman in the middle of the street directing traffic but we were so green we didn't know what he was doing. We decided to get close to him because we knew the drivers would not hit a policeman. But suddenly, all the cars stopped when the policeman made a motion with his arms and hands. We were all so relieved when the cars stopped and hurried across the street. We were just country folks in a big city for the first time.

In Rita's apartment we were given instructions on how to use a flush toilet. We had never seen one before, you see. They told us not to use anything that will plug up the toilet, but since they didn't have toilet paper, they just used newspapers, and the newspapers clogged-up the toilet anyway. Newspapers always seemed to be a source of problems. When I was quite young and living with my grandmother, our toilet was outside. Actually, there was no real toilet; we just went outside, and since we had no toilet paper, we just used newspaper. You should have seen how messy it was when the paper got blown around and across the field by the wind.

I was shocked to find how dirty Manila was, especially the marketplace. In the small towns I came from, although people were poor, their places were basically clean. People weren't so overcrowded and they took care to clean up around them.

We met a guy in Manila whom Pedro knew and who was going to help us get our passport and tickets for the ship. He was a young, good-looking fellow. I remember that he looked very decent and was soft-spoken. He took us to the places where we got our passports and physical examinations. It took several days before we finished signing all the papers needed for travelling and to complete the physical examination. Finally, we bought the passage for the ship and then this travel agent said to us, "Well, do you have some money to change into dollars so you'll have something to spend in America? You can't spend pesos over there, you know." My companions said, "Yeah, we got some money." But I said, "No, I got no money to change." I really had a few pesos, but for some reason, I didn't want to change them into dollars yet. So the others gave their pesos to that guy to have him change them into dollars. He said he'd meet us at the pier where our ship was docked. Well, you know that damn guy never showed-up! I don't know to this day why I didn't give him my money.

It was an especially hot day when we left Rita's apartment to go to the pier. It was April 25, 1926. I remember we had to wait at the pier for several hours before we showed our passports and were allowed to board the ship. The pier was full of relatives saying goodbye to sons and nephews and husbands. None in our group had any relatives there. Rita and her brother were the only ones who came to see us off. When our ship, the *Empress of Asia*, started to move it was already in the afternoon. We went outside on the deck. It was very difficult for me emotionally. As the boat moved out, the Hawaiian farewell song was played over the loud speakers. They shouldn't have played that shit. It was hard enough just leaving everything and everyone you knew. The ship was pulling me away but my feelings were holding me back, telling me to stay. I felt I was being torn in two. I stood on the deck and watched the pier disappear. I stood there until I couldn't see anymore where I came from. But suddenly I recognized the shoreline of Ilocos Sur, my province. I saw the beach of Lapog and the memories flooded back. I remembered that when I was a kid standing on the beach I used to see steamships way out on the horizon going north, but I didn't know their destination. Now I was aboard the same kind of steamship and for the first time I knew the destination. It was hard for me to believe that I was actually on one of those ships and it was me passing by on that steamship. I stayed up on the deck longer than my companions. I wasn't afraid; just a little lonely. I looked forward to going to America to study. That was my plan for years. I kept reminding myself of my goal for going to America: to study, get a job, and save money, and return to help my family. I repeated this thought to myself as we sailed across the Pacific, packed in the tight quarters of the steerage section with a lot of other young men like me. How could I have known then that I would never again see my country, that I had already seen my family, my mother and father especially, for the last time?

❧

I was so naive during that trip across the Pacific. Everything was new and I didn't understand everything that was happening or what I saw. I remember this Chinese who came down to the steerage section several times a day carrying food to sell which came from the ship's kitchen. He would carry the food basket on his head or on his shoulder. As he came by some Filipinos would get on the top bunk, pick food out of the basket without him noticing, and get their food for free. When the Chinese looked in his basket, it would almost be empty. He looked around but nobody moved, and everyone tried to look innocent. It wasn't right what those guys were doing, and being a Filipino, I felt a bit guilty about their behavior. It was years later when I remembered this incident, realizing that the Filipinos in the U.S. played the same role as that Chinese on the ship—one was taken advantage of and cheated by other people. Now how would a Filipino feel being in the same shoes as the Chinese on our ship? Well, pretty soon the Chinese learned their trick and became very careful. Too many Filipinos haven't learned their lessons of survival as well and as quickly as that Chinese.

The trip took almost one month, and since there was nothing much to do on the ship, many of my fellow Filipinos gambled like hell. Back home Filipinos like to gamble—cockfights, cards and *dama* (Filipino checkers)—and on the ship they learned a new Chinese game played with buttons called *sikoy-sikoy*. There was an incident where two Filipinos almost killed each other on that ship because of gambling. They had their knives ready but luckily the crowd separated them before anything happened.

❧

I will never forget the sight of sailing into Hong Kong at night. It was so different from anything I had ever seen before. The electric lights were on and from out there at sea, the city looked beautiful. Seeing the mountains and all the houses that were built right on the sides of the mountains, I was very impressed. The next morning, we went ashore to look around. Right away I noticed the policemen. They were Hindus. They were much bigger than the Chinese, and they carried a big whip. We were just standing around this kiosk and there were lots of Chinese, and out of nowhere, came this goddamn policeman and that son-of-a-bitch just started lashing people with his whip. We just stayed there and watched, so scared we couldn't even move, and wondering if he was going to do the same thing to us. Well, he didn't whip us, just the Chinese, and he told them to get out. That's the first time I had ever seen people being whipped, and I thought to myself that they were treated just like dogs. Before we got back on the ship, I noticed a rickshaw and I said to Pedro, "Look, the one who is pulling is not an animal but a man!"

As our ship left Hong Kong, poor Chinese in sampans came up next to our ship and begged for us to throw them food or money. If the people on the boat threw food that fell in the water, the man on the sampan would just scoop it right out of the water and keep it. Some people on the boat were cruel and threw things that couldn't be eaten, some dirty things. The children on the sampan were tied so they wouldn't fall in the water. I had heard before we left the Philippines about the poor people in Hong Kong, but I didn't expect them to be so desperate and to be treated like dogs. At least poor Filipinos did not suffer like that. Back home, I knew some people who worked as servants in the big towns. They ate, not always the very best food, but at least they ate. Compared to the poor in Hong Kong, the poor in the Philippines seemed to be much better off. The sight of those poor Chinese was also a contrast to my image of the Chinese people because in the Philippines all the Chinese were the merchants and were fairly well-off if not very rich. It had never occurred to me that Chinese everywhere were anything but well-off. Seeing the poverty in China made a lasting impression on me. I couldn't help but ask myself, "Why were some people so poor and some so rich?" Back then I really had no understanding of these things. I thought the reason was simply because some were smart, used their heads, and made money, and others weren't so smart.

We stopped briefly in Shanghai and there I had an even more first hand run-in with poverty. In Shanghai the poor Chinese roamed around in gangs and really tried to take advantage of the innocent. We were just standing around the pier for a while and these rough Chinese guys, young and all of them husky, came toward us. We saw them go up to others and stick their hands right into their pockets, just like that. When we saw this we hurried back to the ship, but they ran after us and tried to grab us. This time I was happy to see a policeman nearby who saw what was happening and came and tore those guys loose from us. Of course then I had no understanding of how poverty and exploitation can affect a person's life, how it can make them rough and commit crimes, or meek, and act like dogs just to survive.

Although we stopped in Tokyo, it was only for a couple of hours so I really didn't get any impressions of that city then. Actually, all I remember is that when we were leaving Tokyo, I was giving some guy a haircut on the ship.

It wasn't until just before we reached Vancouver that I discovered that the ship had a first-class section and that there was dancing up there. At first when we wanted to investigate, we were only allowed to look through some windows. But then, later on, we were allowed to go up and look closer. It was so amazing, right there on the same boat, people dancing in a ballroom. And all the time we had been on that ship, living and sleeping in the steerage section, and even eating our three meals a day in the steerage dining room, we hadn't known that this dancing was going on right above us. It was so nice, the dancers, their nice clothes, in the first-class section, but of course there were only white people. I wondered if that was the way life was going to be like for me in America. I had no idea then how truthful that scene really was to be for me and what as a Filipino I could expect out of life in the U.S.—so close to the good life but always just watching and not being able to really participate.

᳐

It was springtime when our ship docked in Vancouver, Canada. We took a ferry to Seattle on May 17, 1926. When we saw Seattle from the ship, we were all very excited to see the tall buildings all around. It was more impressive than Vancouver and picturesque like Hong Kong. It wasn't until we were getting off that I learned there were about three hundred of us Filipinos on the same ship. When we finally got off the ship, we had to look for our own suitcases. After our passports and baggages were inspected, we finally stepped outside the terminal.

There were a lot of Filipinos there, waiting and meeting relatives and friends who were on our boat. But the four of us had nobody to meet us. We didn't know what to do next. Back on the ship others were always asking, "Where are you going?" Some would say, "I'm going to Detroit," or "I'm going to Chicago," or "I'm going down to California." Some were on their way to New York, San Francisco, or Los Angeles. I asked myself, "Where the hell am I going?" I had never really thought about it. I just thought I was going to America. I was just so excited about going to America that I never stopped to think that America, like the Philippines, had lots of cities. I didn't even really have any idea just how big America was. I had seen maps of it but I had never compared its size to that of the Philippines. So I went down to look at my papers and discovered that I was going to Seattle, Washington. But of course that was just our port of entry. After Seattle I had no plans.

We listened to people talk about what they were doing and where they were going from there. We asked each other, "Where do we go now?" But we didn't know. Just then I saw a *Pinoy* (Filipino guy) walk over to the phone booth right next to me and I heard him ask about vacancies in such and such hotels. I didn't exactly understand what he was doing because that was the first time I heard about getting a room in a hotel. I had never been in that kind of a situation before, you see. So I went over and asked him, "What about us? Is there any place for us, too?" But he answered, "No, it's full but why don't you call this other place, the Diamond Hotel." So I called up the Diamond Hotel and they said, "Yes, we got some vacancies." That was the first time I ever used a telephone. There was one telephone in my home town in Asingan, but I never used it, and when you called over there, all the goddamn stations in towns the wires went through would also ring. In the Philippines only a few people knew how to use the telephone in those days.

We stopped a cab and told the driver we wanted to go to the Diamond Hotel. "There it is," he said when we got there. We paid him, got out, and looked around for the place but couldn't find it because there was no obvious sign, so we just stood on the sidewalk clutching our suitcases and waited for someone to come by so we could ask where the hotel was. But nobody came. It was dark already and we just didn't notice the sign which was high above us from the street. Finally, Gervacio whispered, "*Bayaw* (friend), maybe we go up those stairs." So Gervacio and I went inside and tiptoed up the stairs. But it was hard to see anything because the stairway changed direction, and you couldn't see the top from the bottom. We kept climbing the steps cautiously until we heard people talking. When we got to the top we saw an office and some people standing around. "Who are they?" I asked. "Go and find out," said Gervacio, pushing me to go in.

A girl was behind the desk talking to some people. We went back downstairs to tell our other companions. "There are people up there," I told them. So we all went upstairs carrying our rattan suitcases. We watched and listened carefully to what the other people were talking about with the girl. She was busy, anyway, so we just stood there and listened, looking like puppy dogs. We got closer to the conversation between the girl and a man and realized what was going on—they were talking about rooms. So when she asked us, I said right away, "We need rooms." I was the spokesperson, you see. The girl, a Japanese-American, asked, "How many are you?" I said, "Four." She said, "I cannot give you a room for four people but I can give you rooms for two. So who's going to stay together?" But I said, "No, we all stay together." On the ship and even back in the Philippines we agreed we would never be separated. We all felt that way and especially once we were in America and so far away from home. We were sure we needed some protection. We were so naive. It was not a thought-out plan, more of an instinct. We were in a strange country, we didn't know anyone, so we felt we had to stick together. The girl explained that the rooms were on the same floor. After some discussion, I finally decided to room with Pedro, and Felipe with Gervacio. "How far apart are the rooms?" we asked, and the girl said, "Next door to each other. That one and the one next to it. You'll be pretty close." So we took the rooms.

It was cold and I still felt a little seasick. We had not eaten all night and I felt dizzy when I got to the room and I just wanted to go to bed and sleep. Pedro opened his suitcase, took his blanket out, and covered himself. I took my blanket out, too, covered myself, and fell asleep.

In the morning, we discovered we didn't need the blankets because there were blankets already on the bed. I had never slept on a mattress bed before and I liked it although I didn't notice that it was different that first night because I was so tired. After we got up we went to the bathroom down the hall but we didn't bother putting our pants on and we didn't have bathrobes either. We went in with only our shorts on and there were other *Pinoys* there, too. One of them came up to me and said in a very friendly way, "Where are you from? When did you arrive here in the United States?" Well, I told him my province's name and then just said, "Yesterday." "Well," he said, "here in America, when you go out of your room you put your pants on because that's their way." Then we noticed that everyone we met in the hallway had their pants on except us.

We asked someone in the hotel where we could eat and he told us about this restaurant close to the hotel. That was the first time I had been in a restaurant in my life. We saw some pig's feet in a glass jar and it looked good although we didn't know what it tasted like. We just stood there with our eyes and mouths wide open. The guy behind the counter said, "You want this?" and we all said together, "Yeah." We all wanted the same thing. He put it on a plate and gave us napkins, a fork, knife, and spoon. We sat at the counter and hesitated because we weren't sure if we should hold it with our hands, or use a fork. We had learned how to use silverware in school but we didn't know if it was the right thing to do then. We looked at each other, afraid to start eating. Then the man behind the counter said, "You can hold it. It's all right." He was nice about it. So we picked it up with our fingers and ate.

☙

Everything was new, everything was strange—the food, everything. But it was exciting, and embarrassing too. America was special and so different. America, a place with all kinds of people. The Diamond Hotel, for example, was owned and run by a Japanese. America, to me until then, meant white people, and how surprised I was to find a Japanese hotel in America! Back on the ship I was talking to this white guy and I said to him, "You are an American." Was I surprised when he said, "No, I'm British." Of course we had heard in school about English, Germans, and other Europeans, and of course, they were also white people but it really never sank into my head. I was on a boat going to America so I had assumed that all white people were Americans. Now I was in America and I was discovering that not all Americans were white. I had never thought of that! And the way people dressed in America was different. Even the Japanese dressed like Americans, not like the way they did in Japan as I had seen coming over on the boat.

The girl in the hotel office, for instance, was dressed just like an American girl. She moved more like a guy, you know. In Japan, women acted and dressed very differently than she did.

We also immediately found out that our English was not understood in America. In the Philippines, the Americans understood us just fine. They even pronounced English words with a Filipino accent. But the white guy over here was always wondering if we spoke English or not. We could often understand his questions but he wouldn't understand our reply because of the way we pronounced the words.

When I left the Philippines I didn't know I had friends or relatives in America. But as I travelled around the country, working here or going to school there, I was constantly surprised how often I ran into old friends from the province in the Philippines and relatives too. They just came into my life from time to time. It took me a long time before I could enjoy all the new things I saw and stop feeling homesick. The first few months—perhaps the first year—were the hardest periods for me. But, of course, the longer I stayed away, my desire to go home became less and less. And it was always reassuring to run into old friends and relatives in such a big, new, and lonely country.

My first morning in Seattle I ran into a friend who was my classmate in school back in the province. His name was Alfredo Taban and he said he had been in America a year already. He just came from Cosmopolis, a town outside Seattle, where a box factory was located. He told us he was with some of my relatives who were working in Cosmopolis. I was so glad when Taban told me about my relatives and where I could find them. And I met Taban the second day I arrived in the U.S.! Since we didn't know how to go about and do things but were eager to get jobs like everyone else, we said we wanted to go with Taban to Cosmopolis and three days later, we all went to Cosmopolis to look for my relatives. As we entered the town right away, I saw Jose Sanchez, my father's cousin, who was on his way to work. You can imagine how glad we were to see each other, and he immediately helped us get a job at the box factory. Jose lived and died in Delano. Sometimes I visit him but he is not really interested in what I'm doing now. He was a farmworker and is now very old. He got married after the war and he had two sons—one who went into the Air Force and the other joined the Army.

We lived with my uncle Joe in his apartment in Cosmopolis. It was really a small apartment, a kitchen-bedroom where we did all our cooking which also had a bed in it. There was another very small room, maybe 12-square feet, where four of us slept, and there was no heater. Pedro and I slept in one bed, Joe had his own bed, and another guy had his own bed. In the winter time it was like an icebox in that room because it was on the second floor and there was only one window with a little roof over it. It was so cold that it practically snowed in that room. In the kitchen it was different because there was a stove and that's the way most Filipinos were housed in Cosmopolis in those days.

The day after we got there we went to present ourselves at the box factory. We didn't choose our jobs—the plant manager decided where to place us. Besides the white workers, there were many foreigners who worked there—Greeks, Japanese, and Filipinos. The whites had the most important positions and the Japanese seemed to have the best positions among the foreigners. The Greeks, who were big and husky, were put in heavier jobs. The smaller workers and the inexperienced ones were usually assigned to making boxes except for some Filipino old-timers who had experience operating the machines. But all the young and recently arrived Filipinos began work there by cutting boards and preparing them to be made into box crates which would be used for packing lettuce, grapes and all kinds of produce. That was my first job. We were paid 25 cents an hour, worked a ten-hour day, six days a week. They paid us every 15 days with silver dollars, so my sweater would get pretty heavy since I put my wages in my pockets on pay day. It was a good thing they paid us every 15 instead of every 30 days because I wouldn't have been able to walk home with such a heavy load. I didn't put my money in a bank, just kept it in my room.

The people in the important positions like the managers and superintendents were all white. Their attitude was that you do your work and they paid you for it. As a new immigrant I didn't associate with other workers. The whites didn't care much about us and they regarded us with suspicion. Wherever there were many Filipinos, there always seemed to be many incidents, fights between Filipinos and other groups, usually the whites. We didn't really want to mix with them and they didn't seem to care for us. The Greeks, well, we saw them in pool halls and sometimes we talked to them but usually we just nodded to each other. They spoke their own language and seemed very different from us. There was a lot of tension under the surface between the different racial groups.

When I first started working at that box factory, oh boy, I really cried in the beginning. It was such back-breaking work with long hours. I had never worked hard like that back home. My job went like this: the machine operator cut the wood, passed it on to where a man grabbed it, and piled it neatly in rows. Then I picked up those piles and placed them on a small wagon. That was it but my arms were swollen for a long time in the beginning.

I worked in Cosmopolis from May 1926 until November of the same year, when many of us were laid-off. When the layoffs began, the other Filipinos who still had jobs went on strike at the box factory, the planing mill, and the sawmills. That was the first workers' strike I had ever seen, but since I had been laid off two days before the strike started, I really couldn't join it. I don't know what ever happened with that strike because when I left Cosmopolis five months later to look for work it was still going on.

∽

After going to the States, I discovered that a relative of mine who went to school with me in the Philippines, Godofredo Agbalog, was living in Spokane and we started writing to each other. Now that he was in the States, he had changed Godofredo to Godfrey, but I still called him Godoy like we did back home. He wrote me that he was working and going to school in Spokane so I left the other guys in Cosmopolis and went to Spokane to live with Godoy since I couldn't get my job back at the box factory. I know that my other companions eventually left Cosmopolis too but I don't know when except for Pedro who soon followed me to Spokane.

I remember that April in 1927 when I left Cosmopolis for Spokane because it was still snowing even though it was early spring. I got a job right away as a busboy in a cafeteria and worked there until September when I quit to start school at Lewis and Clark High School. I was able to enter as a junior. I was only able to go to school on-and-off because as soon as I would run out of money, I would quit school and go back and get a job and then when I had saved-up enough money, I would go back to school again.

The next summer of 1928, I was having a hard time finding a job when a group of us who were all looking for work saw an advertisement posted on Main Street which called for men to go to North Dakota and work thinning sugar beets. The ad continued, "Would pay for fare and meals in North Dakota." We signed up right away and that would be the first farm work for me in the United States. There were five of us Filipinos and we left almost immediately on the train for North Dakota. We didn't bring any food with us, nothing except a few clothes. There were some Mexicans on the train who were also going to North Dakota and they had some bread and baloney that had been furnished by their recruiting company which they were using to make sandwiches. They shared their food with us so we ate baloney sandwiches all the way to North Dakota.

Our contract called for two months and stated that we wouldn't get paid until the work was done but it didn't state what our salary would be. We were really just working on good faith but we didn't feel like we had a choice, we had to take our chances since there were no other jobs for us back in the city. All five of us were assigned to work for a small farmer in Manville, North Dakota. When we got to Manville the man from the recruiting company brought us to a grocery store and told the owners to give us food and whatever else we needed. What he didn't tell us was that the bill for all the stuff would be deducted from our pay at the end of the two months. Since we didn't even know how much our pay was going to be they could have told us at the end of the summer, as they just about did anyway as it turned out, that we had eaten all of our wages because all we had left at the end of the contract was $35 a piece.

Our life in North Dakota was very hard. Our job was to hoe and thin beets. Thinning means leaving one plant and destroying the rest around it so the plant would grow bigger and healthier. It was difficult work, bending over and hoeing the sugar beets. We stayed in a small mosquito-filled shack behind the farmer's house. A small pond next to the shack was a breeding ground for mosquitoes. The farmer said we could get our water from the well. I thought the water was coming from underground like the wells we had in the Philippines. But later on we found out that the water came from the rain which first cleaned the roof before ending up in the well. It wasn't even strained and we could see pigeon droppings in the water which ran off the roof. It was pretty dirty water and we didn't fully realize this until almost the end of our contract. Fortunately, we didn't get sick. I think we were very lucky. We had no toilet and couldn't take a bath because there was not enough water. The only good bath we took in the entire two months we worked there was once during a storm. With lightning and everything we went out in the rain and washed. Other than giving us lousy water, the old farmer, whose name was John, was all right. His wife, however, was not very friendly and she talked too much. They were both Germans and had three or four children as I recall. We never once went in their house although we lived right next door, and after work, we just hung around and talked. I didn't play cards so I didn't do very much aside from working in the fields.

Often there was no work for us to do. Now, we didn't know it at the time but we could have gone around to the other farms and gotten some extra work during the off periods at our farm. One day this Mexican saw us just hanging around the farm and he asked why we were not taking advantage of our free time by working some place else but it was too late by then because it was already near the end of our two-month contract. We were just greenhorns, didn't know anything about farm work. Nobody told us anything; nobody gave a shit about us.

John and his wife never asked us to do any kind of work for them except thinning and hoeing and never suggested we could go look for other work. They knew we were greenhorns, that we were from the city by the clothes and shoes we wore. We didn't even have work outfits. The farm work wasn't as hard for me as my job back at the box factory and by this time I wasn't so homesick anymore so that also helped. However, I was continually worrying about going back to school so I could graduate and then I could start helping my family back home. But I wasn't in school then and I wasn't making enough money to send home, either. That continued to weigh heavy on my mind.

After we finished our contract, the $35 we each had left after all the deductions couldn't get us back to Spokane. The recruiting company had paid our fares from Spokane to North Dakota—that was it, only one-way, not round-trip as we had thought from the advertisement we had read in Spokane. So, one of my companions, Agapito Agbalog, who was also a cousin of mine, and I decided to go to Minneapolis, Minnesota, while the three others decided to go to Chicago. Agapito and I picked Minneapolis simply because we had heard about the "Twin Cities"—St. Paul and Minneapolis. But we really didn't know anyone there and nothing about the place. But it was the only place we knew besides Chicago within the distance our money would take us.

It was raining in Minneapolis the day we got there and I remember there were a lot of flies around and it seemed sort of dirty. I immediately didn't like what I saw and I said to Agapito, "I don't like it here. Too many flies. Let's go to Chicago." Agapito agreed so we headed back to the station. But just as we were trying to get back on the train, I bumped into another former classmate of mine from Lingayen, another Agapito, but this guy was Agapito Natividad. I didn't even know he was in the United States. You know, sometimes it seemed like my relatives and old friends were just waiting for me whenever I turned around in the U.S. It got to the point where I wasn't even surprised anymore when I would bump into someone like that just out of the blue. He said, "How come you're here? Where are you going now?" I told him we were going to Chicago because we didn't know anybody in Minneapolis. He said, "Why don't you come to our house?" So we picked up our suitcases and went with him. Again, there was a group of Filipinos renting a small apartment and they said we could stay with them.

In September 1928, I started school again at West High School in the city. I went to high school for so many years that I accumulated a lot of credits. My high school education was very broad, but when I started at West High School, I still hadn't taken some of the required courses for graduation like foreign language.

At the same time I was going to West High School, I was also working at the Dykeman Hotel. I would go to school in the morning and start work at noon. I would get bawled out when I came in late at the hotel by the old lady, the wife of the owner. There were other Filipinos working there and going to school too, and she raised hell about her business being affected by our coming in late because we went to school. But I was able to save enough money to go back to Spokane from working at that hotel.

❧

It was that year that my father died. A letter was sent to me in Spokane and my cousin Godoy forwarded it to me in Minneapolis. Actually my father died several months before I finally learned about it. I was bothered by the news so I tried to keep my mind on my studies. But I could not concentrate. I was always having headaches and feeling physically uncomfortable. I eventually found out that the gas in my room was leaking, probably the cause of my constant headaches. Of course, the other thoughts about my father passing away weighed heavy on me, too. I kept thinking: "Now *Tatang* (father) is dead and *Nanang* (mother) is poor, and there is Leonor and Martin to take care of." After I received the letter about my father's death, I decided to go back to Spokane. I knew I couldn't go home to the Philippines because I didn't have that kind of money. But I wanted to go back to Spokane because the principal at Lewis and Clark High School, Mr. Henry Hart, helped Filipinos with their tuition fees. At West High School I had to pay full tuition, and I figured it would be better if I didn't have to spend a lot of money on tuition so I could send money to my mother again to help her and my brother and sister out.

I read in the letter that my father died in Isabela province. I was told the whole family had moved there in 1926 right after I left for America. They probably moved because of problems with my uncle in Asingan. I'm sure they also chose Isabela because a lot of people in our barrio used to talk about the rich lands of Isabela. The letter about my father's death came from a town called Santiago but I'm not even sure where my father was buried. My sister wrote me a letter that after *Tatang* died, my mother's father went to Isabela and brought them all back to Ilocos Sur.

It was 25 degrees below zero in Minneapolis the day Agapito and I were on the train headed for Spokane. From our window we saw a man walking across a frozen lake. I couldn't have felt farther away from home. I will never forget that sight.

My father, Andriano Sanchez Vera Cruz, and mother married very young; both were around 16 or 17, and they were distant cousins. But there was nothing unusual about this. In small barrios like Saoang, it was quite common for cousins to marry each other, everyone was re-lated in one way or another. My parents were just simple folks. They were not educated. My father could read and write only a little and my mother couldn't write but was able to read a little. When my father would get a letter he would bring it to me to read for him.

I remember that it was my mother who taught me how to speak Ilocano, our native dialect. She taught me how to pronounce the words, how to put several syllables together. She was able to do that even though she had received no formal education. My mother's maiden name was Maria Villamin and just like my father she was born and raised in Saoang. She was a very kind person and people liked her. She was always willing to help. My mother would spend days taking care of a sick relative or friend. My father was like that too. People would always drop by our house just to chat with my father and mother. They both would always lend a sympathetic ear and would always have things to say that made others feel good. They were humble and uneducated but both had a lot of common sense.

Now my uncle Geronimo, who also lived with us at one time, was a contrasting character to my father. He was arrogant and made offen-sive or sarcastic remarks to friends of mine who would come to our house. He even talked that way to my father and his other relatives. He was the kind of guy who always needed to be complimented on this or that if you wanted to get along with him and when he's bullshitting around and bragging you must not contradict him, you see, or else you'll get in a fight pretty soon. He was also a flashy dresser and I think it was because of him that I sort of developed an aversion to dressing up too much or to those who dressed that way. He was like the other side of a coin from my father and I really disliked him. I would often criticize him to my grandmother and she would laugh because she knew I didn't like him. I've never liked people like my uncle.

My mother was very fond of me. She never seemed completely content unless I was with her. She was like a barometer because when I was living at home she gained weight and when I went away to school she got skinny. We were like the moon and the tide. When the

71

moon comes out the tide rises and when the moon is gone the tide goes back down.

I think my character is built upon my parents' personalities. My mother was not a fighter—she was always kind and agreeable and had a lot of patience. Now, I'm like her in that way, I've got a lot of patience too. Both my parents were not highly opinionated people and they never wanted to argue with others. They just wanted to get along with everyone. They also never imposed their own feelings on me and that's why I became independent early.

My father could take a lot but he had a temper. Sometimes he really surprised people when he blew up and lost his temper. Like my father I can also take a lot but I'll blow off steam when I've had too much. I think this is a good part of my personality. I have really surprised people in the union who thought Philip was such a nice guy who always just goes along and then all of a sudden I would explode. Boy, would they jump back when that happened!

∽

When I left the Philippines, I just assumed I would return after a few years with a college degree and lots of money saved. With my first years in the States being so hard, and then my father's death, for the first time I was starting to see that my dreams were not coming true.

Back in Spokane I found my cousin Pedro de la Cruz again. He was working as a schoolboy; that is, he was a domestic helper and was also going to school. He also encouraged me to go back to school. I was able to find a job through a Filipino friend, the head busboy at the Davenport Hotel, the biggest hotel in Spokane. He was approached by a Mr. and Mrs. Amsden regarding domestic help and he told me about it. So I went to work for Mr. and Mrs. Guy Amsden. I was actually hired as a houseboy by Mrs. Amsden whose first name was Rea. Although they were not very rich people, they seemed to belong to the "idle class" and not the working class. They had a very small house and I helped with household chores including cooking and stuff like that. They paid me $2.50 a week for about two hours of work everyday after school. I lived in their house and on Saturday and Sundays I worked eight-hour days. They were not an easy couple to get along with. The husband was lazy and he was very fat. I remember he got tired from bending over. They thought they were aristocratic and behaved so. I was not allowed to eat with them at the table and I had to wait until they finished eating, and then I ate by myself. Both of them played bridge all the time.

While I was working for the Amsdens, Pedro was working for a Mrs. Corvin, a wealthy woman. She was a good woman, very intelligent and a good teacher. I visited Pedro at her house often and I talked with her a lot. One time I was over at her house visiting and I didn't go home until the next day. It was winter and I didn't realize I had to keep the fire going at the Amsden's house. So when I got home, Mr. Amsden was angry at me because he had to shovel the coal into the furnace himself and he didn't like that at all. It was about two degrees above zero that morning and he told me to go outside and shovel the snow off the walkway. Shovel the snow! The snow had already turned to ice! There was no snow to shovel; it was all ice on that sidewalk. I felt Mr. Amsden was being very unreasonable, so I told him I was leaving and went to my room to pack my suitcase. But he said to me, "You can't quit. You work for Rea and you have to tell her. I don't have anything to do with this. She was the one who hired you." But I said, "I don't care if she likes it or not. I'm leaving." So I left, carrying my suitcase to the streetcar stop that went towards town. I had no money. So again I had to quit school. I wasn't paid much by the Amsdens, and I couldn't send money to my mother then. I didn't even have a penny when I left the Amsdens.

I had a friend in town who was new in Spokane. He just came from the Philippines but already had a job. His name was Frank Avecilla, a very nice person, and he lived by himself in a room in a hotel. I went and told him what happened and he took me in and I slept in his room. For meals I went back to the cafeteria where I used to work, Royce's Cafeteria, because they liked me over there. They let me hang around and work and eat there. Mrs. Royce, the owner, ran the place and she was a nice lady. I worked ten hours a day for two weeks in that place but never got paid a penny except for my meals. They couldn't pay me because they really didn't need me. No one said anything about giving me a job but since I was putting in all those hours I was sort of expecting to get paid a little. So when I found out that they weren't going to pay me anything, I quit going there and looked for another job. I found one in a restaurant almost right away as a busboy. I could not find better jobs because there weren't any. I had no education and even those who graduated from college during that time couldn't get good jobs except in restaurants and places like that.

In spring I went to school again, back to Lewis and Clark. I quit the restaurant job and became a houseboy again, this time for Mrs. Maud Long. She was a widow and had another boarder in her house, James Lautit, who was then the chief engineer at the Spokane Water Company. He rarely ate in the house because he always ate downtown, but when he came home, Mrs. Long made sure he had something to eat. Jimmy was a pretty good engineer and his father was a judge in Seattle, Washington. Mrs. Long's granddaughter, Lydia, who was eight years old then, also lived in the house. So there were four of us living in there. We often went places together.

Mrs. Long liked taking me to many places. She brought me to church. She never asked me if I wanted to go; she simply brought me along with her. Jimmy, Mrs. Long and I went to church every Sunday. I remember Jimmy could sing. We also went to the show about two times a week. Mrs. Long had a Buick and she liked to drive it around a lot. When there was a state fair she'd also take me there. When there was a wedding, like one Catholic wedding once, she brought me along to show me what it was like. She also brought me to public lectures.

Mrs. Long was over 50 years old then and she was really a good lady, very different from the Amsdens. Funny how the Amsdens were Catholic and they knew I was brought up as a Catholic but they would not let me eat with them at the same table. Then there was Mrs. Long, a Protestant, who would not eat without me. She cooked and I washed the dishes and she paid me something, maybe also about $2.50 a week. Mrs. Long liked talking to me. Even when I was working around the house, she always wanted to talk to me. She'd get a chair, tell me to sit down, and she would sort of give a lecture, you know. After a while I got very bored with these talks. Soon I really hated these talks because my grades in school, which were pretty good at first, suddenly started going down. Mrs. Long noticed it, too, and she asked, "What's bothering you, Philip? Is it over somebody? Did you receive a letter from home?" She was nice because she cared and tried to find out. But I was young and inexperienced and I didn't know how to be nice about it. I just couldn't say anything. Sometimes she said, "I'll do your work and if you want to go to the library you just go ahead." But I had already made up my mind. I couldn't take it anymore her telling me the same stories over and over again. She was trying to be nice but didn't understand that it was making me sick. I felt I had to quit just to get away from her telling me those same stories.

After I quit Mrs. Long, I went to Pedro and told him what I had done. But he only said, "Why don't you continue school, anyway?" I said I didn't have any money and had to work. He said, "It's all right. I'm working." He was good, that guy. So I stayed in school and lived with Pedro. We finally graduated together around 1930 or '31. And you know, Mrs. Long was the only one who came and she even gave me a graduation present. I was very thankful to her for that. I guess maybe she understood why I left her.

∾

I never ate lunch in school because I couldn't afford it. By one or two o'clock in the afternoon, during physics class, I remember I would get a bad headache because I hadn't eaten anything. Not all Filipinos in my school were in the same position I was in but I just never had money to buy lunch. Ever since I came to America I sent money back home, whenever and whatever I could afford, sometimes $25 or $30 a month. At the time $30 was almost all the money I earned for a whole month. Most of the time though, I earned an average of $10 a week. I started to send money to my mother more regularly after my father died in 1928. Before that the money I sent was to pay off debts for what I borrowed from other people so I could come to America. The average amount I sent home, $25 a month, was equivalent back then to the salary of a teacher in the Philippines.

I enrolled at Gonzaga University in Spokane in the fall of 1931, and because I couldn't afford to pay the annual tuition of $150 all at once, they let me pay only half of it and the rest I could pay at the end of the year. But I never even paid the other half because I still didn't have the money. Again I was sending it all home. I worked all the summer before school began at the university. When school began I continued to work at night in a restaurant, and on Saturdays and Sundays, my days off at the restaurant, I worked at the Spokane Country Club. I was a busboy and also I took care of the men's locker room, cleaning up, making drinks for the men, selling cigarettes, cigars and all kinds of things. I would make about $40 in two days at the Country Club because I got good tips, you see. Saturdays and Sundays were the busiest days when office people, professionals like doctors and lawyers and businessmen came to the club. I worked in that place for a long time so that the members got to know me by name and I knew them too. One of them would say, "You want to give me some cigarettes, Philip?" After I gave him the cigarettes he would tell me to go ahead and sign his bill because he had no time to do it. He'd say, "Sign my name for me Philip," and I did.

It was during my first, and last, year at Gonzaga University, a Jesuit-run school, that I became an agnostic. Here I was, raised a Catholic, coming from a Catholic country and going to a Catholic university, but I was becoming less religious myself. They must not have done a very good job teaching me. However, it really wasn't the fault of the Jesuit teachers at Gonzaga because I've always had an independent mind when it comes to religion. When I was young my mother always talked to me about how I must behave and please don't do this and don't do that because "God doesn't like it that way," she used to say. This always made me very inquisitive about what she was talking about. I understood my father's talk about respect and all that, but my mother's warning against misbehaving and suffering God's punishment as a consequence always baffled me. I felt religious and wanted to believe in something, but then again, I couldn't believe what I couldn't understand. I was a Catholic, but the Church confused me because it wasn't answering my questions, or its answers didn't make sense to me. When I was around 13 years old, I started to go around and visit some of the Protestant churches hoping to find some answers to my questions about religion. I was also interested to find out why, if there is only one God, there were different Christian churches. Right away I discovered that when the Protestants talked about God, sure enough, it was the same God that the Catholics were talking about. And then I learned that many Catholics were changing over to the Protestant church. It didn't seem to me that there was all that much difference between the two churches except the way they celebrated the mass, some of the rituals and some of the things they said and taught about Jesus. When my parents found out about my visits to the Protestant churches, they were very disturbed but they did not say much to me because they always trusted me. Even though I was just a boy then, there were no discussions between me and my parents when it came to religion. They let me do what I wanted to. By the time I was in high school, I had stopped going to the Catholic churches and just visited the Methodist and Protestant churches in my province. I didn't feel a need to go to the Catholic church anymore because I felt I knew what they were doing. I was more interested in learning about these other churches. I would listen carefully to what the preachers had to say. A lot of young Catholics in the Philippines in those days were so devoted to the church that they were overwhelmed by its power and bigness. I just took it for what it was and didn't let it overwhelm me.

It was while I was at Gonzaga that I came up with my philosophy on religion: anything excessive is harmful, including religion. It's similar to the saying that if there's no water, you'll die because you need water to live. But if you fall into a deep river, you can drown too. I argued with classmates who believed in a God who was supposed to be leaned on all the time. For me, to depend on something or someone who's more superior than yourself was a sign of your own weakness and inability to understand what life is all about. This kind of dependence on God makes you more helpless, I argued. I also never liked the idea that the Catholic Church, as other Christian churches did, scared people into believing that giving up their material possessions on earth was a sure exchange for a good and happy life in eternity when no one's even sure what that will be. And I thought the church was hypocritical about preaching that others should give up their material possessions for God when the church was so rich.

To me it may be beyond the human concept to understand God or what the human spirit or soul is. I was impressed by an idea I read somewhere once about the spirit being something that causes matter, that it's a form of energy like the one that produces electricity. Or it could be like some atoms revolving and releasing energy. But I never fully understood this theory, perhaps because I didn't take enough physics classes. I always fell asleep during physics class in high school because of my hunger headaches.

I became a bit of a rebel at this time about religion because I didn't think the teachings of the church were really helping the poor people in the realities of life. Jesus Christ was identified with serving the poor people, yet—and I understood this very well—the church, especially in a country like the Philippines, had been very much responsible for the exploitation and enslavement of my own people! And the people of other religions really competed over who was going to help the poor the most, when in actuality all they did was talk about it a lot because the poor people remained poor.

Anyway, I never wrote anything about my new religious beliefs to my family because my mother was a very religious person. When I was a baby and my mother got very sick her breasts got very sore so she couldn't feed me. My Aunt Fortunata, who was like a second mother to me when I was young, took me from one woman to another, to different wet nurses to keep me alive. My mother made a pledge that if I survived she would pay a respectful visit, sort of a pilgrimage, to this saint whose relic was in a church in a town called Luna, south of our hometown. Well, I survived.

Many years later, when I was around 18 years old, I remember because my sister Leonor was almost two years old at the time, our whole family decided to move to another province to live with my father's mother who had moved before us. The way my family moved to another province was something else, let me tell you! We packed all our belongings, including a *carabao*, a horse, and all our household things, into a boat that was to take us to the biggest port of the southern province we were moving to. It was actually a sailboat for there was no motor on that boat. Two aunts came to help my mother with the move but afterwards they returned to Saoang. The trip was supposed to take a day and a half and we started sailing in the afternoon. Everything went well until we were almost to our destination, when all of a sudden, the wind changed direction. Before we knew it, we were going back where we came from. It was like a storm, that wind, and it scared the hell out of all of us. The waves got bigger and bigger and we were moving away from our port of destination. After several hours going this way, we finally saw land and realized we were halfway back to our hometown. The land we saw was the town of Candon. Upon hearing this, my mother began to wail and prayed and said that it was her fault this whole thing happened. She had not kept her promise 18 years before to pay homage to the saint whose relics happened to be in the town just below Candon.

Although the waves were very big and we were all scared, we made it to shore. I remember carrying my little sister in my arms when we got out of the boat. My mother insisted that the whole family had to walk from Candon to Luna, to make good her promise to visit the saint. The rest of the party went back on the boat after the storm calmed down and proceeded as planned. But we had to walk, my father, mother, little sister, mother's half sister, and myself. We knocked on people's homes when we needed to eat or sleep and were never refused. It was like that in the Philippine countryside. The next morning we finally reached Luna and immediately we went to that church where my mother prayed to the relics of the saint. She was happy and contented after doing that and she said "God and Saint—they made that boat come back because we were passing by here and I had not yet fulfilled my promise. They pulled us back." My mother was like that. Religious and also superstitious. She believed in God and prayed all the time.

I respected my mother's beliefs, no matter how superstitious she might be. However, I wasn't about to write her and only confuse her with my new thoughts. She was happy with the way she saw the world and would not have been able to understand my feelings. I've always been very personal about my feelings, especially religious ones. I feel it's an individual thing: one's religious beliefs.

However, I feel there is a big difference between individual religious beliefs and how churches affect the lives of large numbers of people. As an officer of the UFW, I had to deal almost daily with church people because the UFW has always been very dependent on church support. Cesar himself is a very religious fellow. For me religions and churches are only as good as what they do, not what they say. I was always very supportive of the great amount of church assistance and support the UFW received because it was always given with the sole intent of helping the farmworkers improve their lives and not in promoting this church or that particular religious belief, very altruistic.

The history of the farmworkers movement in the 1960s is not complete without the role of the church and in particular the Catholic Church. You have to remember that when the grape strike started in 1965, about 95 percent of the Filipinos and Mexican farmworkers in the Delano area were Catholics. They attended mass and still do at St. Mary's and Guadalupe churches. The Slavonian, Italian, Irish, and other Catholic growers usually attended St. Mary's Church, praying for more bountiful harvests and profits, for the expansion of their ranches. It wasn't surprising that they believed God favored their prayers because in a few short years many of these farmers became millionaires. Some Filipino and Mexican farmworkers would also attend the mass at St. Mary's, and like other good Catholics, would go to church for moral and spiritual inspiration. However, most of the farmworkers would go to Guadalupe Church which was more conveniently located for them. They were poor and I believed more sincere and honest in their religious beliefs. There was no thought among them of gaining any material advantage over their fellow man. I know the priest liked to see them in mass, but at first, he was scared to look at the *Huelga* ("Strike") buttons on their lapels.

When the grape strike started, the bishop of Fresno was a supporter of the rich growers. The actions and statements he made were in accord with the priests in Delano who at that time were anti-union. That bishop was soon retired but not because of his mistaken judgment, as he should have been, but simply because of old age. However, the bishops that followed him initiated what would be years of strong church support for the farmworkers. The next bishop of Fresno, Bishop Manning, visited Delano and expressed concern and desire to listen to the farmworkers' problems with the growers. His successor was Bishop Hugh A. Donohoe who had been helping to resolve farmworkers' problems even before the strike had begun. He even left two priests, Fathers Mark Day and David Duran, to work full-time with the union.

There were many other church people or groups besides the Catholic Church that supported in one way or another the farmworkers. The Migrant Ministry, which was under the directorship of Chris Hartmire, was the first church organization to give active support and financial backing to the NFWA's decision to merge with AWOC. Representatives of the American Jewish Congress and rabbis came to Delano and discussed with us the ideas of a kibbutz-style community organization, which was very appealing to Cesar. In helping to work out the UFW's jurisdictional quarrels with the Teamsters, the committee that brought the two feuding parties together consisted of a Protestant minister, a priest, and a rabbi who was the chairman. In the San Francisco Bay Area, around eight hundred priests supported and were actively involved in the UFW's boycott of non-union grapes. The nationwide boycott would have never been as successful as it was without the support of literally thousands of priests, nuns, and other church-affiliated people.

In fact, the mediating team that was directly responsible for the signing of the UFW's first table grape contract with the Lionel Steinberg and David Freedman Companies came primarily from the National Conference of Catholic Bishops, the "Committee of Bishops." The chairman was Auxiliary Bishop Joseph F. Donnelly and Archbishop Timothy Manning along with Bishops Hugh Donohoe, Walter Curtis, and Humberto Medeiros were members. Also with the mediating Bishops Committee were Monsignors Roger Mahony, who was at the time director of Catholic Charities, and George Higgins, the director of the Department of Urban Life. Working along with this group was also Reverend Lloyd Saatjian, a Protestant minister from Palm Springs. With this religious and ethnically mixed combination of mediators, the first table grape contract was signed. At the press conference in Los Angeles after the signing Lionel Steinberg said, "I am a Jew and this is the first time that I am being baptized by a Protestant minister and the Catholic bishops. I believe this marks the beginning of mutual understanding between the agricultural industry and the Union for the benefits of both parties." The signing of the contract between Steinberg and the UFW was truly a breakthrough, a historic landmark in the negotiations for table grape contracts, and it only came about because of the tremendous support which came from the churches.

I could list literally thousands of other church-affiliated persons who, in one capacity or another, have assisted the farmworkers movement over the years. I may have my differences with some of the religious teachings but when the churches put their good words into action, as they have with their unyielding support of the farmworkers and the UFW, then I only have the greatest admiration for them. I've always just wanted to be practical when it comes to religion. If a church is helping the people, working for them and with them, then it's good. But if it's not helping the people, then I don't want it.

I couldn't go back for my second year at Gonzaga University because I couldn't afford the tuition and support my family at the same time. So I took a full-time job again at a restaurant and tried to go to night school at the extension division of Washington State College in Pullman. But I went for only one semester and that was the end of my formal education.

It was in Spokane, after returning from Minneapolis, where I again met a very close friend from back home, Frank Valdobino. Although we never had the same financial problems, since his family was not hard-up back in the Philippines, and because he didn't have to worry about sending them money, still we got along very well because we were alike in many ways. Like me he didn't gamble and we shared a lot of common ideas. He was a helpful, sensible, and honest guy, and he always acted properly and never embarrassed me as a friend.

Both Frank and I worked at the same restaurant in Spokane after I quit Gonzaga University. It was a pretty good job and we had been there a while but one day Frank got into trouble with the assistant waitress who was supposed to be in charge of us. She and Frank got into a fight over something but Frank said, "Oh yeah? Well, fuck you!" Her name was Pauline and she was Italian. She didn't know how to deal with people very well and was always saying sort of impolite things, although I don't think she was aware of it, or was really trying to push you too hard. So she said to Frank, "I'm going to tell Ruby," who was the head waitress. See, I think maybe Pauline had asked Frank to do something that Frank didn't feel it was his job to do. So Frank said, "Go ahead, tell Ruby, you goddamn. . . ." And he was so upset he also said, "Fuck Ruby too!" He turned to me and said, "Come on Philip, let's get out of here." So there we were. But Pauline said, "Don't go Philip. You should stay; we like you and Ruby likes you." But Frank was very close to me. We were like brothers. Our relationship was so strong that I had to be on his side, if he was right or wrong. So I left the restaurant with him. We quit the place and prepared to go to Chicago. That was in 1934 and that's the way I left Spokane.

Frank and I talked about going to Chicago several times. We heard, you see, that some Filipinos in Chicago were working in the post office and that sounded like a good job. We wanted to try and see if we could get work like that too. So we took the train to Chicago. When we got there, as it turned out, there were no jobs. It was true some Filipinos worked in the post office which was a good paying job then. I knew one guy who was getting $35 a week at the post office while we were only getting $12 a week at a restaurant job.

Walking around Chicago, I used to see ads for jobs that read, "Help Wanted, No High-Waisted Filipinos." The high waist, the zoot suit, was in fashion in the 1930s because the picture shows had made them popular. I guess the ads said that because guys who wore those zoot suits were looked upon as hippies during that time. They were not considered serious workers but guys who were just out for some fun. It was actually just another way for the employer to discriminate against Filipino workers if he wanted.

Of course a lot of guys wore those high-waisted suits then; they were very popular with the Mexicans too. But the Filipinos really looked funny in those clothes because they were so short, even smaller than the Mexicans. The Filipinos always liked to dress up, to look nice. Whatever was in fashion, well, they'd wear it no matter how it made them look.

Frank and I stayed together and rented a room in a hotel near downtown. Frank was walking around town one day and when he got to the corner of Randolph and Clark Streets, this old guy, Weiskopf, the co-owner of the W & R restaurant, saw Frank looking inside the place to see if he should go inside and ask for a job. Weiskopf just said to Frank, "What are you doing here?" Frank said, "I'm looking for a job, sir." Weiskopf looked him over and said, "O.K., you come tomorrow." Just like that! Frank went back the next morning but the old man had forgotten all about him. Frank had to remind him about the day before, what he told Frank about the job. Weiskopf said, "Oh yeah?" Suddenly, he took off his big bus coat, handed it over to Frank, and told him to start working right away. The old guy was like that. If he liked you, he liked you. He didn't spend his time finding out about who you are and this and that.

I didn't start working with Frank at the W & R right away. One day the old man asked Frank if he knew of another good boy like him to come and work at the restaurant. When Frank came home he told me that I had a job too. Although we sometimes worked as busboys our usual job was making coffee, cutting cakes and pies, and making soda and shakes. We worked alternate shifts so when Frank was on I was off and vice-versa. We worked at the W & R restaurant for seven or eight years, the whole time we were in Chicago. In fact, it was the only job I ever had in Chicago. Working with Mr. Weiskopf for such a long time, I got to know him pretty well. He told me that he didn't go very far in school and had worked before as a dishwasher and a waiter. He was a good businessman and did very well for himself and his family. All his children became professionals, one a doctor, one a teacher, and another had a business administration degree. I liked Weiskopf. He was a fair man to work for.

There was this Jewish guy who ate a lot at the W & R. His name was Maurice Landisman and I remember him telling me that he was a socialist. I think he was well-off and his brother taught at the YMCA Central College. Maurice and I talked a lot—he seemed to like to talk to me. I told him that my problem then was that I wanted to continue my college education but that I didn't have any money. I asked for his advice. He told me that possibly he could make some arrangements at Central College through his brother so I could get my tuition waived. I know he tried very hard to arrange it but it never worked out. I still had my ambitions of finishing college. But going to college would have meant working less than full-time and that wouldn't have provided me with enough money to send home. So I finally gave up my ideas about finishing my education. I continued working at the W & R restaurant until the war and was able to send money home on a regular basis.

Although by the start of the war I had been around the labor market for many years, I was never aware of the possibility or even the need to organize workers such as myself. I was too busy surviving and helping out my family in the Philippines. It wasn't until I moved out to Delano from Chicago because of the war and became a farmworker that I found myself with time to educate myself more about politics and economics for the first time since I arrived in the U.S. I also no longer had to support my brother and sister in school. They had finished school, had good jobs, and were able to sufficiently take care of our mother. This took a lot of pressure off me. So by this time I found more time to read about politics, economics, and workers movements, and it was only then that I found an outlet to do something meaningful for myself as well as for my fellow workers, and that was joining a union.

Like I said before, the UFW changed my life. In spite of the many problems that were present from the beginning, I nevertheless devoted myself to the UFW for many years.

"I sacrificed too much . . ."

The struggle over leadership in the UFW has always been a sticky issue. Some people don't want to discuss it, but I think there are important lessons to be learned from it if the issues are understood and discussed properly. It's not a black and white issue, you know, Filipinos versus Mexicans. The conflicts over leadership have occurred just as much within our own ethnic groups. Many good and sincere Mexicans have had to leave the UFW and form their own splinter unions in places like Texas, Florida, and Arizona because of deep-rooted disagreements and misunderstandings with Cesar or Dolores and others in the leadership. Among Filipinos there were similar problems. In AWOC, before the merger, Ben Gines and Larry Itliong were always sort of competing for the number one spot in the leadership although it was never a hostile thing between them because they were able to continue to work together. But people knew there was this conflict between them. I never had ambitions like that so it was easy for me to work with both of them although I was closer to Ben than Larry at that time. For me, the important thing was always to be able to help and if helping meant serving as an officer of the union then I'd do that. I didn't care who was leading the union as long as he was honest and doing some good to make the union move ahead.

As an officer of the UFW since its inception, I had the opportunity to observe the inner workings of its leadership. I had learned to become a good observer from childhood when I had to tend to the family's *carabaos* because my father was too sickly to do this job. I was usually the only boy among a group of men doing this work, and I listened to the older men's stories and noticed their habits while we all watched our *carabaos*. I noticed how people interacted with one another, and whether they got along or not, and in the union I was able to continue this kind of observation.

Whatever happened to the Filipinos in the union, or to the Filipino farmworkers in general, is a question you don't hear being asked or read about in books about the farmworkers movement or the UFW. But I think it's a question worth asking. It's not easy to answer, though, but maybe if I tell you my experiences and observations as an insider in the union, and then later, as an outsider, perhaps some of the answers will be found.

When my group of Filipino men came to America in our youth, we felt a great deal of uncertainty. We lived through the Great Depression on top of other hardships due to the color of our skin. Filipino women did not come with us when we immigrated so many of us felt quite lonely here. When we looked for female companionship, we came up against racist laws and attitudes. Our thinking and ways of seeing the world were greatly affected by our colonial-ruled cultural attitudes which originated in the Philippines. All this, I think, resulted in our developing complex personalities and heightened insecurities. Becoming a part of a union with other nationalities wasn't easy psychologically for Filipinos. While some of us were basically shy and would rather not be put in front of other members during union activities, and that's the way I was, there were also some Filipino leaders in the early days of the UFW who acted just the opposite: they smoked big cigars and dressed-up like somebody with money. Some even displayed their money in the front shirt pocket in a big roll so people could see it. They bullshitted around a lot, usually with the more uneducated workers who would be impressed by this appearance and hope that this flashy guy would help them out here and there. Even if there were only a few Filipinos who behaved this way, still the impression tended to be over-generalized by other people, making it more difficult for the majority of Filipino leaders who were working honestly and without pretensions to achieve united goals. So it was too often half-truths about Filipinos and their leaders that created misunderstanding and which actually got me into trouble within the leadership circle of the union.

You see, as an officer of the union, I had to speak occasionally in public although ordinarily I didn't like to be chosen for this task. Perhaps this was a weakness on my part as a union officer. But there were times, however, when I had no choice: I had to speak for the union, and during these times, I believed my message was important enough and that I was presenting it in an interesting way because I could see that the audience was interested in what I had to say. I'm from the "old school" when it comes to public speaking, which means I deliver my talk with a lot of enthusiasm. I guess you call it a bombastic style and I think some people liked to hear me for a change. But some union leaders didn't like it as much. I guess they felt challenged simply because my audience reacted so favorably when I gave a talk in my own way. So after a while I noticed that some union leaders started excluding me from major decision-making. I was shocked by this kind of reaction at first because I was never interested in taking away anybody's position in the union hierarchy. Yet the misunderstanding or miscommunication existed and it was very difficult for me to put an end to it or change it. I've always known I had great limitations as a leader and strongly felt that other leaders were more capable of doing what I couldn't handle. I don't think Cesar ever felt challenged by me, but I know that some of the Mexicans and Filipino officers felt that way. This may all seem very silly now, but unfortunately, that's what happened at the top levels of the union. I suppose it's not different than in any other group. Many well-intentioned union officials became afraid that I would try to challenge their positions. It's really a shame. One of our biggest struggles in the UFW was how to get rid of these kinds of feelings which were usually rooted in misinformation, half-truths, and years of poor communication between different ethnic groups. I only realize now how important and also how difficult the struggle was within the union to overcome these kinds of problems.

Among the Filipino officers within the UFW, Larry Itliong was the most effective because he had authority, some real power. When he was the assistant director, next to Cesar, he had the authority to decide who will get $5 for this and $10 for that, who could get some extra money, and who can have his car fixed. Larry was recognized and given that power because Larry always fought hard for what he wanted. But because Larry was an aggressive and forceful leader, as was Cesar, it was obvious that eventually there would be problems between the two. In the early days of the union, Cesar could not afford an open confrontation with Larry when they differed. Cesar had not yet consolidated his power completely, and the Filipinos were still an important force in the union so Cesar could not keep Larry from having the authority he wanted. But as years went by, the role of the Mexican within the union increased while the role of the Filipino diminished. Everyone could also see the problems between Filipinos and Mexicans worsening. The growers and the Teamsters constantly tried to capitalize on our differences through their propaganda while many of us in the UFW leadership tried to improve the situation. Since Larry was the most visible Filipino leader, he was always in the middle of these controversies.

It's difficult for me to admit, but in retrospect, it is true that the Filipino leaders in the UFW have been more showcase than anything else. Larry was an exception because he had power and authority for a while. He was the kind of guy who felt it was important to be up-front during the meetings, but not just to show his Filipino face among the leadership, oh no. Larry had real responsibilities and he met them head-on. Unfortunately, Larry left the union. He wasn't kicked out, no, he left on his own. I knew he was very frustrated because he was trying to be an effective leader but was always resisted by Cesar. That was not his only reason, though. He also quit because he felt he didn't get enough support from the Filipinos themselves. For example, when Cesar preached austerity with the limited union funds, Larry cooperated by being very selective about who was going to receive financial assistance and he didn't necessarily favor Filipinos over Mexicans. He just tried to be fair. But this was disappointing to his own people. It was selfish of some Filipinos to think that just because Larry was one of their own, that he would turn his head when it came to them and let them by when others had to sacrifice. Then they would not support Larry enough and naturally it got very frustrating for Larry. Later he blamed the rank-and-file Filipino for not supporting the Filipino leaders in the union. He was correct about this. Larry also complained that the advisors to Cesar had too much power and were discriminating against some union members. He often complained that the Filipinos were losing their voice in the union and he was correct about this also. So I know that Larry suffered a lot of frustrations and that's why he finally left the UFW. And I think it was due to these frustrations that he made some mistakes in judgment in the last few years before he passed away. It seemed to me that during this time he aligned himself with the Teamsters and allowed himself to be used by the growers in their campaign to try to destroy the UFW. For this, many people would never forgive him. He even voiced support for the martial law government in the Philippines. This was wrong for a great labor leader like Larry to do because the Philippine government had banned labor organizing and strikes in their country at that time.

Larry did a hell of a lot for his people, but often it was his own people who let him down. Sure, he made mistakes and it's important to talk about them because there are important lessons to be learned for future leaders. Our survival in this country as a minority is determined by how well we learn from the lessons of the past. Since Larry died many Filipinos who didn't even know him that well are now trying to build him up as a Filipino hero, as the founder of the farmworkers movement and stuff like that. Well, there were a lot of contradictions about Larry and I think it's more important to understand the whole situation in which Larry played a role than to just build him up as a hero. For me we need the truth more than we need heroes.

We had a testimonial for Larry and many people came for a variety of reasons. Some of those who came I know even disliked Larry but at the testimonial they said nice things about him. Well, you know how these things are. The Filipinos in Delano obviously had mixed feelings about Larry, but we collected $20 a person at the testimonial and gave Larry's family $5,000.

I had visited Larry before he died. I wanted to see how he was since he had been pretty sick and just talk about old times. We had not seen each other for quite a while. He had quit the union while I had stayed on, and although in our hearts we were still friends, it was difficult for us to just get together because of politics. I told Larry then, "Our (Filipinos') role in the union has not been written and sometimes even intentionally deleted because the Anglos who wrote the story didn't know all the facts and we didn't speak up." Larry agreed with me and wanted to talk to me about many things we had never talked about. But he said he had to leave the next day to go to San Francisco to see a doctor and when he got back we would get together. But it was too late. When he came back to Delano he passed away shortly thereafter. I have felt so terrible about this. The first time we could have really talked and it was too late. The Filipino leaders in the farmworkers movement should have tried to be closer, to be friends and talk more about our mutual problems. Our unity in the union was always very weak because we never got together to discuss things. We always went our own ways, had our own pride. This wasn't good for our unity. Now Larry is gone and the rest of us will also be gone soon, and most of our stories will die with us. And we only have ourselves to blame.

After Larry died I thought a lot about the closeness of a Filipino family and community that was now long gone among my generation of Filipinos in the U.S. I couldn't help remembering the small barrio of Saoang where I was born where everyone was close to each other and everyone helped each other. Those who didn't were very much criticized. Helping others was something that was taught to very young children. Older people would say to the kids, "When you're well, you'd better remember to be helpful because when you're sick you're going to need others to help you, too."

When I was very young my grandmother took me to live with her. She was my father's mother, a very affectionate lady and I loved her very much. My father was her only child by the grandfather Vera Cruz who died when my father was still young. My grandmother remarried and then sent my young father to live with his grandmother who then raised him. So when my grandmother took me—I must have been two years old—it was sort of to replace her son whom she gave up to be raised by her own mother. She remained very close to my father in spite of the separation. Her taking me in was like a family tradition because my father was also raised by his grandmother, you see. It was hard for my mother to give me up like that to my grandmother. I was not returned to my family until I was seven years old. My father didn't want me to go either but the idea was not as bad for him because it was his mother who was taking me. It was also harder for my mother because my younger brothers who were born after me—all four of them—died shortly after birth.

Living with my grandmother when I was very young was an important experience for me. It showed me that my family was a strong unit; all family members shared in the responsibilities of the family. When I had to go away to high school and live in a boarding house, it was my grandmother again who took the responsibility and came with me, stayed with me in the boarding house, cooked my meals, and washed my clothes. I became so close to her because of these different experiences that when my family moved into my grandmother's house I even slept with her in her room.

I value this tradition of the extended family very much and oh, how much we have lost in the U.S. as a Filipino community without this tradition. Back home it didn't matter who chose to join the family as long as that person showed sincere feelings towards the family. Then everybody in the family accepted that person as a member. I remember a neighbor of ours, her name was Isla, and she was much older than my parents. She wasn't a relative, just a friend but she would always come over and talk and would stay late into the night. Although she had a big house next to ours, which was much smaller, she would often sleep over at our house. She had children and neighbors who were her own relatives, but she was also accepted as part of our family.

The idea of the extended family even goes beyond the family to the community and becomes a very good attitude of community consciousness. Helpfulness, understanding, and loyalty. Oh yes!, these are the better traits we Filipinos brought with us from the Philippines. However, all the good traits we brought with us and all the good traits we were taught America had to offer, from the day we got off the boat, had been slowly destroyed by the harsh realities of our life here. The anti-miscegenation laws made it difficult for us to raise families. This cruel situation denied us the right to live a normal, respectable life. As men without families in the U.S., it was hard then, and even now, to just get together among ourselves as though we were a family. Although our experiences brought us close together for survival reasons, at the same time, we let go of our sense of community that we felt in the Philippines. It was easier for each of us to go his own way the longer we stayed here. To a certain extent if we hadn't done this, if we had stuck together closer instead of growing apart, perhaps it wouldn't be as difficult now to tell our story. We wouldn't have been so pulled apart by several forces so successfully. But I still believe in those Filipino traits that I learned when I was a young boy in the Philippines. I don't want the young Filipinos here in this country to forget that these good traits are part of their heritage and that they should strive to reestablish them.

Since Larry died I have realized that my greatest mistake, my biggest shortcoming as a union officer was not fighting like hell for what I knew was right. I took the passive role too often because I had learned from the past struggles in the Filipino community how bad fights at the top can get. I always sacrificed my personal convictions for what I thought or was convinced was the good of the union, and sometimes I think this was a mistake. I just sacrificed too much. At the same time, because I was not a forceful officer and didn't try to push my ideas I've survived in the union. I was a nice guy and nobody paid too much attention to me. Other officers in the union would often confuse an attempt to push your ideas with the desire to push yourself to the top. I know others felt threatened by Larry, mistaking his forceful methods of fighting for ideas as an attempt just to rise in the leadership hierarchy. Nobody ever felt overly threatened by me except from the little notoriety I received from speaking in public and, as I said before, I was sure surprised how quickly the other union leaders reacted to that. However, within the union's hierarchy, at board meetings, or talking with other officers, I always worked very hard to be consistent to the principles that we had been fighting for since the beginning of the union. I am still respected for that—it's really all I've got. Sometimes when talking to the public, I would have to bend a little and not say exactly what was on my mind. I just couldn't come out and say in a public forum that I disagreed with Cesar over this or thought some policy of Cesar's was not fair or democratic. As a union officer, I always had to consider the overall integrity of the union, and sometimes this meant tempering my public voice. But in private it never made any difference to me who I was talking to in the union hierarchy because I never hid anything there. What I believed I would say to everybody because that's the way I am.

You would be surprised how two-faced people in the union's hierarchy were, and especially when there's just a little temptation like a free meal here or something else there. I never said anything to make people follow me or take me to the chop suey house. I know I wasn't very well-liked by some board members because there were times when I just wouldn't compromise. I always tried to be flexible and if an issue didn't mean compromising a fundamental principle too much, then I'd go along even if I wasn't in full agreement. But if it was something I thought was very important, I would refuse to cooperate and would not throw in my vote with the rest just to make it appear on record that it was unanimous. At times I strongly disagreed with the board members and because I stood strong and refused to give my O.K. to a proposal that I believed was not good, some board members reacted by isolating and removing me from their ruling clique. I used to think my stubbornness was a strength for me but some have said it is my weakness. Well, I think it was only a weakness when I used it at the wrong times.

During the grape strike of 1965, the board wanted me to go and work on the boycott. This would have meant going away from Delano and working in other cities to organize the boycott of certain products like grapes and lettuce. I didn't want to go. Some of my reasons for not wanting to leave Delano were personal and some were for what I felt was the good of the union. I didn't feel that I had to tell the board members my personal reasons, but I did tell them those which related directly to the operation of the union. That's the way I am. Even if my personal reasons were extremely important, I just couldn't bring them up in front of the board. I always tried to keep my personal life separate from my role as a vice-president of the union.

You see, I had my house and property and I didn't want to leave Delano for a long period of time because no one would look after them. Working for the union, I got paid $5 a week, plus something for the most necessary expenses like food and gas. I didn't have money saved up, and I was too old to go back to work in the fields so I felt that I should stay around and manage my property to make sure it would be O.K. so I wouldn't lose it. It's my small security for the future, for my retirement after I left the union, and it's better to have that than nothing at all. This was the one thing I didn't tell the other board members. I just didn't feel that it was any of their business. Many of the union officials looked down on you if you had some kind of personal security outside of the union. They said the union was our home and that the union would take care of you. But that's bullshit. Some of the strikers were losing their houses and the union didn't do anything to help them out. The Filipinos have always had a hard time getting assistance from the union when they really needed it. I had fought as long and hard as anybody for the union, but I also knew that the next day Cesar could kick me out just like that. If that happened then I would have to take care of myself.

The reason I gave to the board why I wanted to stay in Delano and not join the boycott team was that I felt I could help the union more by staying in Delano. For example, I felt that it was more important for me to attend board meetings because then I would know what was going on in the entire country or all over the world regarding the union. But if I had been in Chicago working on the boycott, I would only be communicating from there to the central office. That would not be good because, remember, Filipinos were a minority in the union, and we needed to be well-informed about what was going on. As second vice-president, the highest ranking Filipino officer in the union, it was my job to try to keep the Filipinos as well-informed as possible. One of the major reasons that there had been problems between Filipinos and Mexicans was due to poor communication. I felt it was my job to help smooth out these misunderstandings and I sure as hell couldn't do that if I was out in Chicago or some other place. Communication had never been good, especially between Cesar and other Filipino leaders, and since Cesar and I got along fairly well, putting me in a far-off city was only going to make things worse. This is what I told Cesar and the board members.

When all the officials involved in planning the boycott went to Santa Barbara to discuss plans, I asked Cesar if he still wanted me to join, knowing I wouldn't go away from Delano. He said yes, he wanted me to be in Santa Barbara. So I went. But from that day on, the other officers learned that I had a strong will and could be quite stubborn in my own way. I'm my own person and I guess this independent attitude sort of alienated me from the other board members.

I always wanted to speak my mind during board meetings, but I couldn't do this easily because, whenever I expressed a different opinion from that of the group, I felt the reaction was suspicious, intimidating, and even insulting to me sometimes. I felt the differences of opinion, especially by those in the minority, were usually taken as being against the union itself. That's why I was always in and out of the leadership clique all at the same time. I didn't want to be totally controlled by the union leadership—that was very important to me—but I also tried to work within the union as best I could without upsetting the whole show.

Although my frustrations in the union were basically the same as Larry's, unlike Larry, I had resigned myself to accepting the few responsibilities that the board charged me to perform. But even when I was given full responsibility for something, the board was still very reluctant to give me full control. In the UFW power was held by Cesar alone, and he handed out some power to individuals at his direction. I want to be as honest about this as I can possibly be. I'm not going to criticize Cesar for holding on to the reins of power when he did it in a fair and reasonable manner. It was no easy task leading a farmworkers movement, and Cesar had to be tough and even authoritarian at times. And we should only admire and praise him for his successes. But there were also times when I think Cesar became blinded by his power, and the best example I can think of, that I was personally involved in, was in regards to my position on Agbayani Village. Let me tell the story and I think you'll see what I mean.

❧

The idea of building a retirement village came from Cesar. He was smart to see right away that it was a good idea. He knew that the village would do a lot to consolidate the support for the union and especially support from Filipinos. However, when the concept of the village was first discussed, it was just a long-range plan. We had to continually postpone starting the construction because the union had so many other priorities. In the late 1960s, the UFW had not won its contracts from the growers yet so we were really busy just fighting for our survival as a union. We were fighting the growers and the Teamsters; we were organizing the boycott at the supermarkets trying to keep consumers from buying non-union products; and we were on the picket lines too. It took a tremendous amount of time to solicit people's money through donations and recruit volunteers to help on the picket lines and with the boycott. And we needed volunteers to help in the office. So Agbayani was conceived as an idea long before we finally got around to it.

It wasn't until after the union's first convention in 1971, when officers were officially elected for the first time and we had finally won contracts with growers, that we had the time to plan the retirement village project. Ramona Holguin, a UFW volunteer, came and worked with me and she was able to recruit Luis Peña, a Chicano architect, to make the drawings for the village. Ramona was a very good worker and very persistent. Agbayani Village was designed as a 60-unit home for retired farmworkers. It was decided that the village would be located on the east side of Forty Acres. It would be the newest building on the entire Forty Acres compound which already had the Hiring Hall, Health Clinic, offices, and, of course, the gas station. The design provided each tenant with a private room and an adjoining bathroom. This was a much-deserved luxury in retirement that farmworkers have had to do without all their lives. In addition, there was a central kitchen, dining hall, living room, and recreation room which later on was furnished with a pool table donated by volunteers who brought it all the way from San Francisco in the back of a truck. The entire building has central air-conditioning, an unheard of luxury for farmworkers who spent endless summers bending over ten hours a day in scorching hot fields from one end of the San Joaquin Valley to the other, where a temperature of 100 degrees was normal. And it would even get as high as 120 degrees! Outside was a large garden where the tenants would grow many of their vegetables and fruits. It was decided to name the village after Paolo Agbayani, a Filipino who died from a heart attack while he was on the picket line in Delano in 1967.

When construction finally began in April 1973, over 2,000 people were involved in building the village, but because of limited funds, the structure was built almost exclusively by volunteer labor. No more than a half-dozen or so people were ever paid and they only received the standard $5 a week plus expenses from the union. People came from foreign countries just to help out with the construction, from Canada, England, Switzerland, Germany, France, Japan, and many others. Hawaiian, Japanese, Chinese, Filipino, and Black Americans, and many others from all over the U.S., came to help. Building the village was a wonderful experience. I learned from working with all the young people that their generation is much different from mine. They understood the importance of our struggle here and made their contributions by working in Delano as volunteers on the construction of the village. I'm sure they'll never forget that. The construction of Agbayani Village was quite a remarkable achievement which all those associated with it should be proud of. The building has earned compliments from local contractors who have told me that it is probably the best built structure in the entire San Joaquin Valley.

When the village opened in 1975, the union decided to have a two-rent policy for the retired farmworkers who would live there: $67.50 a month for those original strikers who never went back to work and stayed with the union, and $80 a month for those who just moved in from outside. Even those who joined the strike in 1965 but had left the union in ensuing years, maybe because of financial reasons, or for whatever personal reasons they may have had, would pay $80 a month to live in the village. I was against this, and along with some other Filipino old-timers in the union, like Willie Barrientos and Celedonio La Cuesta, argued that this was not fair.

First we argued that the rent was too high. The old-timers could live cheaper than that in town where they would be closer to the stores, the pool halls where they traditionally liked to hang out, and to their old friends. We felt it was only being honest to mention that the old-timers liked to hang-out at the pool halls; it was the reality of the situation of their culture and old age. But Cesar and the board didn't want to hear about it. To them the idea of UFW farmworkers playing pool or gambling was sacrilegious. Cesar too often has had an antiseptic view of farmworkers that has narrowed his perspective, and I think caused him to make incorrect decisions.

In addition, we argued, why discriminate against old men and charge them an additional $12.50 a month until they die just because they didn't stay with the union continuously? Many left because the union had no money to help them out and they had to eat too. Well, the board said we had to charge that much rent to pay-off the costs for construction of the village as soon as possible so the union could build another retirement village. This really made us angry and we were against it. Let me explain something to you about the village and the union.

Remember, the Filipinos were a minority in the union and a lot already felt discriminated against by the Mexican-dominated union. Sometimes they had been right and sometimes they had been wrong about this. But what is true is that the union definitely had made some mistakes when dealing with the Filipinos. Remember also that most of the farmworkers who were near retirement or even long past retirement age were single Filipinos. They were the ones who had been in the vineyards the longest, and therefore, they were the ones who would be the first to live in Agbayani. These old-timers had worked for 50 years. Most of them hadn't had a decent place to live in since they came to this country. Most of them had no families; they never married because of discriminatory anti-miscegenation laws. Unlike the Mexicans who had plenty of their own people around, and could even go back to Mexico if need be, the Filipino would have had to go 8,000 miles across the Pacific to find a Filipina to marry. Some of them had just stopped working in the fields for the first time when they came to live in Agbayani, and they were 70, 80, and even 90 years old. These were the old Filipino workers who were used by Cesar and Dolores Huerta to establish funds for a retirement home from the first table grape contract signed with Lionel Steinberg.

We told the union board: "If you charge this high rent, you won't fill-up the place, and if it's not full, then you won't pay it off as quickly. And why are you considering building another retirement village if this one is almost empty? Why should these men be entirely responsible for paying for the construction of this building with their rent when most of them will be dead anyway in just a few years?" Agbayani is a nice place but no matter how nice it is, if the old-timers couldn't afford it they wouldn't come. So we told the board again, "If you lower the rent just a little bit, it would be easier to invite retirement-age farmworkers to the village, fill it up, and then the union could pay off the building even quicker. But the board just didn't listen to us and the two-rent policy was enacted at the originally proposed rents. After about two years the place was still only half-full.

At that time I was the second vice-president of the union, only Dolores Huerta and Cesar were above me, but I was a Filipino. I was supposed to be in charge of Agbayani. Cesar himself had put me in that position. Up until I left the union, all the residents at Agbayani except one Chilean lady, one Mexican, and an Anglo who had since left, were Filipino old-timers. I went to the board again and told the board members that these old-timers can't afford to live there when they can live cheaper downtown. I tried to explain that these guys want to be able to save just a little money to pay for the maintenance of their cars, to visit relatives and friends, and little things like that. Maybe they could save just enough so they could visit their relatives in the Philippines just once before they died. I asked the board again, "Why are we discriminating against these old-time Filipinos?" But they still didn't listen to me. So I was pretty mad. Shit! They wanted me to tell my people this and that, to put them in line when they did things that didn't look good for the union. They wanted me to be a leader. I was put in charge of Agbayani, but then on an important issue, they wouldn't listen to me. So, for me, it became useless to fight for the authority I needed to carry out my job. I knew that the board and Cesar just weren't going to let me have my way. I wasn't like Larry, I didn't want to fight with Cesar all the time and anyway, usually Cesar showed pretty good sense. But sometimes he didn't.

The Filipinos have bent over backwards to accommodate Cesar. Larry did it and I had to also. And here was an issue that didn't mean that much to the union but was very important to the Filipinos, and, for the sake of harmony within the union and just respect for those old-timers who did so much for Cesar in the beginning, you would think that Cesar could have given in to my proposals. However, no matter how upset I was about this I never took it outside the board. That's just the way I am. I would never publicly challenge those above me and it's really the only reason I survived for 12 years in the leadership of the UFW.

I'm afraid, now as I look back, that this kind of attitude that was perpetuated by Cesar really came out of a fear of losing power. Along with Cesar, those on the board would tell me to go here and go there, do this and do that but they also made sure that I was never given any real authority, so that I could never have real power and possibly compete for the prestige and leadership that they so cherished. And God, maybe Larry scared them because he did challenge them for the top jobs. But I never did and still they were scared.

My position on the union's executive board after the rent issue started deteriorating. It was becoming extremely frustrating for me to the point that I was even finding it difficult to make sound judgments during board meetings because I wasn't being informed about a particular issue we had to vote on until the time of the meeting. The others would have already been discussing the issues together before the meeting and all of a sudden at the meeting I would be asked to participate during the final making of a decision. But I hadn't been given the information I needed so I could make a sound judgment. Decisions should be based on all the information that you can get your hands on. But if you are only given the facts at the board meeting at which that particular issue is to be voted on, well then, you're in a bad position. They would tell me that a decision had to be made right then and I had to vote either "yes" or "no." I wasn't the only one being treated this way. It was the same for Pete Velasco, the other Filipino officer. But Pete would just go along and vote "yes" if they wanted a "yes," and "no" if they wanted a "no." Well, that's the way Pete is and I'm not going to criticize Pete; he decided to accept that situation for his personal reasons. But this whole situation of just being used as a rubber stamp really turned me off.

Since the central office had been moved out of Delano to La Paz,[4] it became much easier for me to be excluded completely from the inner workings of the union. But even when the central office was still here in Delano, there were important issues discussed that I knew nothing about. Sometimes I'd hear about them only through rumors or I'd read in the newspaper what was going on behind the scenes.

Now on the other hand, as a Filipino officer, it was important that my communication with the Filipinos within the union be good, and this was also difficult because over the years the Filipinos had become suspicious of their leaders. Because in the past their leaders hadn't always been honest with them, they did not trust their leaders, or anybody for that matter, who stood up in front of them and tried to get their votes or support. They had become overly cautious from years of being used and manipulated. There was a time when they looked up to Larry, but many were eventually disappointed by some mistakes Larry made. When he finally left the union, the Filipinos felt deserted and they wouldn't trust him anymore and were generally suspicious of any

Filipino in a leadership position with the union. Many of the Filipinos in the union acted like dogs who had been badly mistreated by their masters. Although they stayed with that master, their suspicions of being treated unfairly were high.

In regards to me they felt this way and that way. They could see I had no power so they knew I couldn't be a real leader. But they always respected me for my principles which all of them knew I continually stuck to. You know, it's difficult sometimes for me to make the Filipinos understand, especially the older ones. I would speak to them about this and that but they often wouldn't understand all that well what I was talking about. They were very set in their old ways. And there were certain subjects that I didn't really feel free to talk to them about, certain things that they had become quite sensitive about. For example, many old Filipinos at the village spent their time playing cards all day and how could I say to these old guys who are 70, 80 years old, "Why don't you get out under the sun and do some little things like help clean-up around here so people can see that we are doing something for the union?" like the board suggested. There were those on the board who didn't like it when visitors would go to Agbayani to see the famous UFW retirement village and some of the old-timers were sitting around playing cards. They'd say to me, "Philip, you should get those Filipinos off their butts sometimes to show that they still care for the union and want to help around the village here and there." Well, it's sort of understandable that some of those guys just didn't want to work anymore for anyone, even the union. They'd worked all their life and now all they wanted to do was play cards. And what was wrong with that—they were very old. However, there were always a few guys who did things for the union to help out around Agbayani, and they did these chores without anyone asking and they did it until they died. Some of the Filipinos also had their roosters, their fighting cocks, and they kept them behind the village. It takes time to care for these roosters. To them that's serious business, an important pastime which is deeply set in their Filipino heritage. The union wanted me to tell the old-timers to get rid of their roosters if they were going to live in the village, because they use them for gambling and it looks bad for the union. But hell, I couldn't do that. That's all they had and the union wasn't being sympathetic to their needs in old age.

There's another problem in dealing with the Filipinos that I have been aware of for many years and it goes back long before their involvement with the union. Many of the Filipinos in the union wouldn't even come to a meeting if you called one. They felt it was a waste of their time. And then the ones who came would get all excited about the Robert's Rules of Order although they were not properly acquainted with these parliamentary rules of procedure. Of course these rules were made to help facilitate and not disrupt the meeting. In a normal business meeting if a guy has to wait to talk because he is out of order he doesn't feel insulted. But you do that to a Filipino and right or wrong he'll want to fight you. Sometimes, it got almost unbelievable, nothing could be accomplished because some guys got so hot just about the rules of procedure.

This wasn't just a problem in the union. It happened and still does to this day all the time out in the Filipino community. It is not uncommon for the election of a president of some organization in the community or even the choice of a beauty queen to end up being decided in court with hired lawyers for the opposing parties. And all this just to sustain a defeated candidate's supposed rights, ego, or false pride. Both sides end up broke and the community loses its unity, trust, and faith among its members. And I can see that this immature behavior on the part of the adults has turned off many of the younger Filipinos from getting involved in their communities or with the UFW.

In my position on the board I always felt like I was sitting on the tip of a double-edged sword. Both sides had responsibilities. The union should have been more careful to deal fairly with its minority members. Filipino leaders like Larry and myself should have been given more authority. You can't expect the Filipinos in the union to believe in the union if they see that the Filipino officers are only a showcase. The Filipinos aren't that dumb. They realized that this attitude reflected on how the union leadership saw them too. But on the other side of the sword, the Filipinos could have been more organized and more supportive of the union in general. It's a very difficult problem and one that has not been solved properly within the UFW.

❧

When I joined the union and got involved in the Delano strike in 1965, my sister wrote me that my mother was very sick. If I hadn't joined the union, I would have gone home to see my mother. Even though I hadn't seen her for almost 40 years, I was still her oldest son and she missed me very much. But the farmworkers movement was very demanding at that time and since I joined the union I was always broke. So, I never again had the chance or enough money to take the trip back to the Philippines.

In 1972 my mother died. I found out about her death from my nephew who lives in Cebu. My nephew went to Mindanao for the funeral and wrote me about it. My brother and sister only wrote me very recently about her death, maybe because they didn't want to shock me.

Well, my feelings about my obligations to my family were divided. I knew I had done my job to support my brother and sister to get a good education. I had sent them thousands of dollars from my wages here to help them get where they are now. I felt I could rely on them to protect my mother, feed her, house her, take care of her. She was just as much their mother as she was mine and they felt the same obligations and love I felt. But it was hard for me when I heard about her death because I was her oldest, and even after all these years, I still felt the pull, and maybe the guilt, of leaving so long ago and never being able to go back.

I loved my mother very much. Everything I did in this country was for her and my brother and sister. Sometimes the sacrifices we made in this country and especially for this movement were much greater than many people realized.

"A minority within a minority"

If you look back over the history of the UFW, you can see that all that has been written about the union has been focused on the Chicanos, the Mexican workers, and all the resources of the union that were spent in organizing were done for the Chicanos. All the churches that have helped the union have really been working for the Mexican workers, not the Filipinos. The Filipinos, as the major minority in the union were left out. Even if they showed some unity with the Mexicans in the beginning there was no real effort to keep them organized and close to the union.

In the early days of the union, just at the time of the merger, there were probably more Filipinos involved with the union than Mexicans. Now, I don't know the exact numbers but what is important to remember is that the Filipinos were a large group within the union then. But quickly the membership of Mexicans grew because of Cesar Chavez's leadership and the large number of Mexican workers in the state. The union, year after year, became more and more Mexican-dominated, and the Filipinos became a smaller minority. If you start with a group of Filipino workers who really don't grow in numbers over the years and then the growers start bringing in Mexicans and the number of Mexican workers increases rapidly, then the Filipinos obviously will feel challenged by the Mexicans. And it's not just the growers bringing in the Mexicans. With a poor, underdeveloped country bordering on a rich developed country, it's obvious that the workers are going to come pouring across the border looking for a better life. There is always going to be that feeling of conflict and competition between two minority groups of workers when there is such an imbalance in numbers. Many of the Filipinos were becoming more labor conscious and were understanding how this process of bringing in a new group of immigrants to replace an older, more established group worked. They had come 40, 50 years ago and now they could see it happening again but this time they were the old established group being replaced. So naturally the Filipino, whether he did or didn't understand what was going on, felt the pressure and realistically feared for his job. It was the growers' game to keep the workers at odds this way and to have a supply of new immigrant laborers who would work for lower wages.[5]

A natural hesitancy developed on the part of the Filipinos to cooperate with the Mexicans, and because of this, the union had many problems getting the Filipinos to participate in union affairs. The union wanted the Filipinos there—their membership, their presence, looked good for the union. How could it be the "united" farmworkers union if it was only Mexican membership? But Cesar and the others weren't willing to put the same time and money into organizing the Filipinos as they did with the Mexicans. There was this general assumption that the Filipinos would be there, cooperate, not ask questions, and somehow this would just work out magically. As a union officer I just couldn't say to the Filipinos, "This whole farmworkers movement was started when the Filipinos sat down in the fields in Delano, so you guys should come and support this and that now." It just wasn't that simple.

Filipinos had many bad experiences in the past when it came to meetings, so just because it was a UFW meeting, why should they be any more excited about attending? To make matters worse, the UFW meetings were dominated by the Mexicans, so often the meetings were conducted in Spanish, and sometimes union officials would forget to translate. The Filipino doesn't speak Spanish; he speaks English, and often not so well. And of course he speaks his native language from the Philippines, which for most of the Filipino farmworkers is Ilocano. At the union meeting the Filipinos always had a difficult time understanding all the things that were said. This enhanced misunderstandings and increased the mistrust. Because the Filipinos as a group were few in comparison to the Mexicans, they found it difficult to speak out at meetings. They were embarrassed by the language problem.

Another issue that created friction was the allocation of money. People who came in and worked for the union would always face financial problems. The union paid us only $5 a week plus basic expenses. When a Filipino and Mexican were faced with some financial problem, the union would help the Filipino last, if at all. So, Filipinos often left the union just because they had money problems. When I finally left the union, there were only two or three of us Filipinos left in the union office, and I know that when it came to pinching pennies, it was the Filipino who got left out.

One of the worst problems in the union between the Filipinos and Mexicans came about because the Filipinos felt that there was unfair dispatching going on in the Hiring Hall. They felt that the Mexicans were dominating and only giving jobs to Mexicans. Well, actually I don't think the Filipinos were always right about this complaint, but this issue was a very complicated one.

When the UFW was formed many of the Filipinos who joined had been working in the same labor camp and under the same foreman or labor contractor for many years, even up to as many as 40 years for some. Many of these Filipinos lost their seniority when they joined because the growers wouldn't cooperate in supplying the needed information the UFW needed to establish proper seniority rankings. You can imagine how confused and upset the Filipino felt. They joined the union after working at the same farm for most of their lives and all of a sudden the union took away their seniority in that farm. They felt they couldn't trust the union after that and many shifted over to the Teamsters. The growers, always afraid of the potential strength of the UFW, and in particular of Cesar's charismatic leadership, had intentionally upset the seniority lists and then would give Filipinos back their seniority when they went over to the Teamsters. The Teamsters were cooperating with the growers' dirty tactics in order to recruit workers away from the UFW.

I know that the UFW tried to do what was right for most of the workers, Mexican or Filipino, but in the beginning, there were mistakes made here and there and it had become very difficult to make up for some of these mistakes. It was rare that the union people didn't try to do what was right in the Hiring Hall, but one of the problems in properly dispatching workers was that the union had to depend to a great extent on the cooperation and sincerity of the ranch foreman who worked for the grower. Many of these guys were Filipinos who had been around a long time. Their job was the highest position a Filipino farmworker could expect to get. Some of the other races, like the Japanese, had gone on to become small farmers, or in a few cases, rather large ones. But most of the Filipinos didn't or couldn't save their money, so the foreman or contractor's job was the top of the ladder for them. In that position you had to play the game with the growers. When it came to hiring, well, of course their interest was mainly in getting the men the growers liked. Naturally they also tried to propagandize the workers they hired to believe that the grower they were working for was the best, and that they couldn't find anyone better. These Filipino foremen or labor contractors would also usually remind the Filipino farmworkers that the UFW was a Mexican union and the Mexicans were going to take away their jobs.

These Filipinos working for the growers as foremen or contractors saw the UFW as a threat to their job security which had taken them many years to get. The union wanted to break up the power that these middlemen held over the hiring and firing of the worker. The UFW wanted to make the hiring of a worker a more equitable and clear-cut process that was controlled by the union and not by some easily manipulated or bribed individual who would be under the direct influence of the grower. This situation historically went back many years.[6]

I think that it's kind of interesting also that often it was the Filipino mestizo who was closest to the grower and ended up getting the more financially rewarding position of foreman or labor contractor. It seems that there was a racial thing going on. The Filipino mestizo is lighter-skinned than the other Filipinos and I guess the white grower felt more at ease with someone whose skin color was closer to his. Of course, no matter what the color of his skin was, the grower used the foreman or the contractor to help manipulate the workers.

It could be very frustrating for the worker. He would go to the grower and the grower would say, "I can't hire you because you have to go to the UFW Hiring Hall." Then when the worker started to go, the grower would say, "But if there was no UFW around I could hire you right now." Then maybe the Filipino did go to the Hiring Hall and he couldn't be hired immediately because there was a seniority list and so, how would he feel?

In addition there was an agreement between the grower and the union that when the grower needed a worker, he had to give the union a work order. But then to confuse the situation the grower would send the worker back to the Hiring Hall but wouldn't send in a work order to the union. The union couldn't dispatch someone if they didn't have the work order. So, the worker is back at the union Hiring Hall asking to be assigned to his job but being told by the union that he can't report to work.

And then the grower had one more game to play to confuse and frustrate the worker and try to damage the UFW. When a worker would report to work after the proper work order had been filled, the grower would just refuse to hire the guy if he had been sent by the UFW. When this would happen, the union would use all its legal resources to force the grower to pay the worker, but this could end up in a long legal fight, and in the meantime, the worker wouldn't get his job or his money. The grower was being a real devil.

At the union meetings, officials would try to explain what was happening, so the union members would not be confused and blame the union. The union had to work hard to maintain the workers' confidence, Mexican as well as Filipino, through those trying times, that it was working for their best interests. But when the union official forgets to translate the message or explanation into Ilocano about what was happening, what the union was trying to obtain for the worker, how the growers were trying to sabotage the progress the union was making in fighting for equitable hiring and working conditions, all the time speaking in

Spanish only, then it's not hard to see why many Filipinos felt lost or left out.

Language was a crucial factor here. The growers had the Filipino foreman or contractor who would always speak to the Filipino in his native tongue, put his arm around his shoulder when he talked to him, which is a traditional Filipino gesture of friendship, and was always quick to reach into his front shirt pocket and pull out a couple of dollars if the Filipino farmworker needed a little extra cash to get by. The UFW just wasn't going to break its back for the Filipinos. With only two or three Filipino officers, there was just no way that we could make the personal contact that was necessary to all Filipino farmworkers who felt cheated by the union. Cesar really wasn't that concerned about the loss of a Filipino here and there to the tactics of the growers and the Teamsters since he felt it was the Mexicans who would make or break the union, not the Filipinos. Cesar could see the trends as well as anyone. The Filipino rank and file in the union was much older than their Mexican counterpart. And the Filipinos weren't being replaced by younger blood. The post-World War II Filipino immigrants, and especially the Filipinos coming to the United States starting in the 1960s, were mostly people with trades and professions. Very few of them were coming to work in the farms. It was just becoming a matter of fact that the era of Filipinos playing a major part in the farm labor force in California was coming to an end.

In 1970 I wrote an article for the progressive paper, *The Catholic Worker*. My optimism and early idealism with the new union were reflected in my comments at the time such as this one: "In the farmworkers union all races meet and join together to achieve an ideal: mutual understanding, sincere cooperation and true brotherhood. The farmworkers movement in Delano is the closest approximation of the ideal that I have seen in many years. My hope is that our unity and brotherhood will be permanent."[7] Today, although I still believe in the same basic principles I realize that the problems associated with turning those principles into reality are much greater than I thought they would be. Larry Itliong had feared, without voicing it publicly as a union issue, that the organizing of Filipinos would be de-emphasized if not outright ignored, and because of this, the Filipinos would end up feeling discriminated against by the UFW and just generally left out. One of the more subtle yet outward demonstrations of this are the UFW slogans. They reflect how the Mexicans, being the majority in the union, became very ethnocentric. When they called out "*Viva La Raza,*" or "*Viva Cesar Chavez,*" they didn't realize that all these "*Vivas*" did not include the Filipinos. As a matter of fact, they didn't include anyone else but themselves. That, of course, turned off many Filipinos and the other smaller minorities within the union, like the Blacks and Arabs. The Filipinos especially didn't like it when the Mexicans referred to themselves as "Chavistas." Terms like that, you see, are not inclusive but divisive.

"The movement
must go beyond its leaders"

The issue of democracy within the union was for me probably the most controversial and difficult to deal with. I was always idealistic and envisioned a workers' organization that put democracy and equality of opinion above anything else. But as the UFW developed, it grew to be far less democratic than I had originally expected. However, I am not so naive not to understand that this entire issue of democracy is not just a black and white situation. Many of the Filipinos just quit the union because they didn't feel they had an equal voice. They criticized me and said, "Philip, why do you stay; you're powerless, you're just being used." Larry saw it that way and his decision to quit was quite clear. But I also knew that in the UFW I had a voice, if only a limited one which I wouldn't have had if I was outside the union. I was able to speak to workers of all races and to people from all over this country and the world. The union was the vehicle that provided me with that opportunity. At the same time I had to fight a personal battle within the union to defend my belief in democratic principles which were constantly being challenged.

As a young union the UFW had to learn from its own mistakes and from observing the mistakes of bigger unions. In the beginning the union had to deal with the most undisciplined and uninformed group of workers because they were new to the whole process and their politicization was just forming. You could see this when you went to the meetings. That's why at first everything in the union was just oriented to building the workers' morale. The union used a lot of slogans that became famous and well-known internationally, like "*Viva Cesar Chavez,*" "*Viva la causa,*" and "*Sí, se puede.*" In the beginning the workers weren't spending their time analyzing the issues so they could completely comprehend why they were putting their time and efforts into the union. No. Instead, a lot of time was spent developing slogans, and the workers just took for granted that what their leader said was true and good for them because they trusted their leader completely and he was saying, "*Sí, se puede.*" In a situation like that I understand that you need a strong leader who can make the important decisions, but if it's going to work and really be beneficial, then whoever is on top has got to be honest beyond reproach.

As a result, we had a general membership that wanted to fight for the union, but at the same time, became very dependent on following instructions. It's important to understand the stages of development of the farmworkers consciousness. It's similar to the growing stages of a child in relation to his parents. To become a truly democratic union, some kind of a transition has to happen. Just like with the parent and the child, as the child grows up, the parent allows him to have more responsibilities. So as the workers become more knowledgeable about issues affecting them the union should give them more to think about and resolve which would really start to make it a more democratic union. But for a long time, the rank and file of the UFW only went along with everything Cesar wanted. When I would tell them what Cesar wanted they would just take it for granted that I was telling them something that was good for them. It wasn't as if they were developing the ability to judge the virtue of something for themselves. They just assumed it was O.K., for their benefit, because Cesar had said it was.

One major problem that I saw develop out of this in the UFW was that Cesar was seen as so important, so indispensable, that he became idolized and even viewed by some followers as omnipotent. I have been invited to speak at many different universities and often Chicano students who have heard so much about Cesar asked me if Cesar was really a democratic leader. As an officer in the union, I was bound to defend the union when I was at a public forum and to uphold what Cesar was doing, so I always had to temper my personal opinions. But to a certain extent it was true that the union and especially Cesar did not conduct themselves in a truly democratic manner. But one thing the union would never allow was for people to criticize Cesar. If a union leader is built up as a symbol and he talks like he was God, then there is no way that you can have true democracy in the union because the members are just generally deprived of their right to reason for themselves.

In the beginning of the union, I think it was permissible to see a leader that way. To draw the membership and the supporters, the leader has to have the personality to put these different elements together. That's the only way the movement could succeed, I think. And Cesar did attract the workers and people outside who could help and work for the union. Cesar had the ability to get them to work without forcing them, but by kind of getting them on their own free will. Cesar had this wonderful charismatic personality, integrity, and honesty that caused people to want to support him and his causes. That's why Cesar was very successful in building the farmworkers movement into a real union. It appeared to the public that Cesar Chavez's honesty and integrity were beyond reproach but I would not be honest if I didn't mention that in practice it wasn't always true.

The UFW had many volunteers, mostly young Anglos, who came to help the union. These people devoted a lot of their time and energy working for the union and I think that they had a good influence on the union. The UFW is a unique union in that it was able to get active volunteer support from outside the actual membership of the union on the local, national, and international levels. The boycott, for example, was based in cities around the United States and all over the world. And these were not farmworkers alone who were responsible for the success but also students, church people, professionals, housewives, and other labor unions in countries as far away in Europe as England, Sweden, France, and Germany. You have to give Cesar a lot of credit for this. It was his charismatic personality that attracted these volunteers, this non-union support. Cesar also had the ability to get people to donate their money and support us in different ways, like not buying products produced by growers who were against the union. There are many people worldwide who even today, although many things have now changed, and the union has signed many contracts with big growers, will still not drink Gallo wine because they remember it was called, "the blood of the farmworkers." They remember Cesar on the long march and Cesar on the hunger strike.

Cesar put himself right up in front. He put his life on the line sometimes and would never ask a worker to do something that he himself wouldn't do. It was hard for people to forget that and it caused them to develop an extreme devotion to Cesar. Another guy in Cesar's place would have done things differently and may not have been as effective as Cesar. I tend to be of the belief, however, that even if Cesar hadn't been there, that the conditions would have created the necessary leadership.

Some volunteers spent so much time with the union and played such an important role in union activities that they started to see the UFW as their union too and I think rightly so. Some of these volunteers just didn't sit back and accept everything that Cesar and the board said. If they saw a policy or situation that may have needed changing or improving, they would question it and wanted to discuss the matter. Many volunteers who came to help the union, and were put in positions that required responsibility, ended up feeling very intimidated because they were not allowed to participate in any decision-making and were just asked to follow orders. And if they didn't follow orders that sometimes didn't seem fair or proper, well, that was it, they had to leave. Well-intentioned volunteers were kicked-out by Cesar without a word of explanation. Some of these incidents were ugly, and the volunteers were usually hurt and humiliated. These incidents too were often over minor misunderstandings. The leaders of the union have never wanted to talk about these aspects of the union and even the better books on the UFW have not mentioned them. An ex-UFW volunteer, Michael Yates, who is a college professor, has written an article about these unfair firings.[8] It is good that someone isn't afraid to write his feelings because it's important that more people understand this issue. These incidents, of course, may be exceptions, but they have happened and there was never any discussion whether Cesar's actions were right or wrong. Cesar and some of those close to Cesar can be ruthless, and Cesar has made his biggest mistakes by assuming that he is the only one concerned about the future of the union. Because of this attitude he has punished or fired individuals who were loyal to the union, based on false or inaccurate reports.

This kind of undemocratic policy greatly hurt the union and I feel that it was this kind of attitude by the union leadership that was responsible for closing the Huelga School.

The school was originally created by the union for the children of union members—from nurseryschool age to about third-grade or maybe a little higher. When the school first opened an Anglo woman named Sarah was put in charge. However, the school got into such financial difficulties that after a while even Sarah thought they might have to close down the school. But Chris Hartmire said he would try to get the Migrant Ministry to finance the school. Chris is a Protestant minister and he organized the Migrant Ministry to help the farmworkers. The Migrant Ministry took over the operation of the Huelga School from the union. Although it was still considered part of the UFW, this was merely an unofficial association because it was now actually run and financed entirely by the Migrant Ministry for the use of the union.

The teachers in charge changed often because the pay was so low and the young teachers could only volunteer their time for so long. Here was another situation where very dedicated young Anglos came to help the union. They devoted their lives for a time to help the farmworkers and asked for nothing in return.

After Sarah left Steve Manson took over. Steve had been a regular teacher in Delano public schools but he was interested in helping at the Huelga School. But there always seemed to be difficulties between the white teachers and the Chicanos, and I think this is another reason why the white volunteers didn't stay longer. Soon after Steve took over from Sarah, before we knew it, Steve was being accused of this and that by some Chicano leaders in the union. Cesar allowed the accusations to be made, but he wouldn't allow some sort of a proper hearing to clear the air and let people hear both sides of the story. Steve was so hurt by these accusations that he left. The next teacher to run the school was Shelley Spiegal from Los Angeles. Shelley was a very nice person and a good teacher. Shelley hadn't been there too long when here comes trouble again, this time from Dolores Huerta. Dolores would say to Shelley, "You aren't doing this and you aren't doing that," and so on. Dolores wasn't a trained teacher and wasn't there everyday with the children. I knew Shelley was doing a good job because I heard reports from other people. Why Dolores decided to go after Shelley was not clear in the beginning because her criticisms were not based on professional reasons. Dolores criticized Shelley for petty reasons. And here again, the union leadership allowed this to happen. It seemed obvious that Dolores was doing this simply because she did not like the idea of having a white teacher for the Chicano kids. The Huelga School was mostly Chicano children, you see. It didn't matter even if the Anglo was a good teacher. So what does this say about the union leaders allowing this thing to happen. It's pretty sad because the situation showed the union to be no better than the whites we all know about who are against having their children taught by non-white teachers. And here was Dolores Huerta, the No. 2 person in the UFW to Cesar Chavez and one of the most famous and important Mexican American women in the U.S., acting the same way.

Chris Hartmire resisted this time because there had just been too many problems with the Chicanos in the union making life difficult for the Anglo teachers at the school. Chris said to Dolores at a board meeting, "Dolores, why do you interfere? Shelley's O.K." Dolores came back with, "The Huelga School is still part of the operation of the union." And since Dolores was an officer of the union she felt that she had some right to say who ran the school.

I think Dolores was dead wrong. That kind of question should be left up to the entire board. Here again, you could see the problem of Dolores, just like Cesar, thinking that she was the union herself so she could just make any decision she wanted. That was very dangerous. Dolores and Cesar are just an incidental part of the movement; they are not the movement themselves.

It seems to me that after the entire board had made its decision, then it should have been presented to Chris and the staff of the Huelga School. It was the Migrant Ministry after all that was paying for the school, not the union. Well, they finally had a meeting and Shelley was allowed to stay for the time being. But you could see that Dolores was unhappy about the decision and I knew that there was more trouble to come.

At the following staff meeting in Delano, Dolores started attacking Bob Ream right out of the blue. Everyone was really surprised. There had been no basis for what Dolores was saying and then, just like that, she fired Bob right there at that meeting. Now this is what you have to understand. Bob is an Anglo and he and Shelley were good friends. Bob had originally been a volunteer for the union, and then he was hired to work for the union on the construction of Agbayani Village. Bob was one of the most important people involved in the construction. He was paid by the union the standard salary of $5 a week but what he gave the union over a period of years is too great to be measured in time and money. Even after the village was finished and the people had moved in, Bob continued to volunteer his services, even though he was off the payroll. Bob was a very capable and handy young man and provided the union with unreplaceable service. He was a quiet, soft-spoken guy. Everyone liked him very much, just an extremely nice young man. He was no radical and in fact wasn't that interested in politics per se. When Dolores fired him at that meeting without a proper hearing it was just to get at Shelley. Well, what could Bob do? He knew he couldn't fight Dolores. He was really hurt, so he walked out and Shelly walked out too, and soon after that incident, the school closed down. So now, there is no more Huelga School and the union lost the services of two of its best volunteers.

Cesar and I never agreed about these arbitrary firings, and there had also been a lot of red-baiting associated with some of these firings. It's kind of ironic because the growers always tried to hurt the union and Cesar personally with red-baiting tactics. The growers used to try to link Cesar with Saul Alinsky because they mistakenly thought Alinsky was some kind of a communist. But then, Cesar and Dolores and other union officials turned around and used these same low tactics against some union supporters.

The way I see it, one of the basic principles of the farmworkers movement is that it should include everyone who wants to help. If someone comes to destroy the movement, then you have to kick that person out, of course. But you still have to be fair about it, have a proper hearing, and take a legitimate vote. But so long as they help, you don't ask them, "Are you a socialist or a Democrat or a capitalist?" You don't ask questions like that. These firings have hurt the union tremendously. We have lost the support of many good people because of these tactics. Cesar should broaden his views about the union and some of its supporters. He should not be so allergic to other people's politics. I have been the only one on the executive board who objected to these firings. I oppose these kinds of firings because I think that if you want a democratic union, then the democratic process should apply to everyone.

Cesar played the political power game because he wanted to build a strong union. To direct a young movement that was vulnerable to attack, a union like the UFW, Cesar believed he had to have a collective leadership but with a lot of personal control. Cesar was a good leader, he had many good ideas, he seemed to really care for the workers. He came from the working class and he fought like hell for the workers.

But on the other hand, Cesar's importance became a dangerous thing. Leadership, I feel, is only incidental to the movement. The movement should be the most important thing. If the leader becomes the most important part of the movement, then you won't have a movement after the leader is gone. The movement must go beyond its leaders. It must be something that is continuous, with goals and ideals that the leadership can then build upon. But who can predict what an individual leader will do? Just because the leadership was good in the beginning doesn't necessarily mean it will be good forever. Sometimes a leader's success will block his ability to look at the broader view. Maybe later on Cesar will start thinking more and more about his own pocket book. Or maybe he will become very conservative and demand that "this is what we have to do," even though it goes against the basic principles of the movement. As it stands right now, if something happened to Cesar, then the people wouldn't know where to go because the union is now too tied to Cesar's image, very much so. If he quits or passes away, it will really shock the union. Dolores Huerta may be a strong leader but she cannot fill Cesar's shoes. Richard, Cesar's brother, cannot replace him either just because they've got the same name.

◡

I have been using the terms "union" and "movement" almost inter-changeably. Everyone in the UFW, everyone who has been associated with Cesar Chavez has. But actually, when I stopped to think about it, I realized that this is very dangerous. Movements and unions are really two different things and because of the way Cesar is, the two have been mixed together into what is probably not a very positive combination. Movements have charismatic leaders who are not necessarily democrati-cally elected. Unions also often have charismatic leaders, especially dur-ing their early stages, but they should always be democratically elected. In my opinion a movement is more an idea, a philosophy. A union is a democratically formed legal entity that has a very specific function. Cesar is the head of the movement, the farmworkers movement, and he is also the head of a union, the UFW. He can't continue to wear both hats forever, or it will eventually work towards the detriment of one if not both of these groups. The UFW is only a part of the farmworkers move-ment; it isn't the entire movement. The movement existed long before there was a Cesar Chavez or a UFW and it will exist long after. But as it is now under Cesar Chavez's leadership, sometimes the farmworkers movement is the UFW and sometimes the UFW is the farmworkers union. It cannot continue this way forever. I think it is time that Cesar decided who he is and what he wants to do and not to try to do two things at once.

It just got to the point for me where Cesar's omnipotence as a union leader became unacceptable for me and Cesar could not afford to have someone like me around because, although most of the time I went his way, sometimes I didn't believe in what he was saying and therefore wouldn't support his position. Representing the minority membership of the union, I had always tried to balance things out. I believed that the union should have been more democratic but I also knew that Cesar had to be a strong leader because the union was young and it could have easily been attacked and destroyed. At times when I felt strongly that certain things should be said about the union, and had to be said in public, I said them, but always with great care and tactfulness. But this was never received as constructive criticism from one who was an important part of the union and who cared for the union. To Cesar and the board, a contrasting opinion, voiced publicly, was not to be tolerated.

"Pounding me with their anger"

I spent many years with the union fighting for the rights of farmworkers. I stayed with the union long after the other Filipino leaders told me I was a fool to hang around. But see, I have always believed in the struggle of the farmworkers, although I am not always in agreement with the leadership of the union. I have many differences with Cesar Chavez, but my support of the farmworkers, the rank and file of the union, hasn't changed.

However, my frustrations in the union increased every year and my body was no longer strong enough to support the ideas I had in my head. I was always the lone dissenting vote on too many key issues, so I had been considering leaving the union for some time. You know, I feel that younger people who are stronger must come and continue our struggle.

I finally decided to tell the board that I was leaving the union leadership at a meeting just before the union's 1977 convention. This would be the best time, I thought, because the union would elect new officers at the convention, and I wanted to get out before the elections so it wouldn't seem like a big deal. I always tried to keep my differences with the union's leadership away from the public because I knew that internal struggles that get unfavorable publicity outside can be harmful to the farmworkers movement in general and the union in particular.

You see, at that meeting when I told the board members I was leaving, I thought they would all be glad to get rid of me. But I was surprised by their reaction. Right away they got excited and said that I should not leave the union. Then following my brief announcement, Gilbert Padilla, the secretary-treasurer of the union, just like that, said he was leaving the union too. I was really surprised, maybe even more than the other board members, when I heard Gilbert say this. Gilbert was sitting right next to me and maybe the other members thought we had planned this together, but we hadn't. I did not know what Gilbert was planning and he didn't know what I was planning either. But just like that it seemed like we were together and everyone was looking at us.

They asked Gilbert right away why he was leaving and Gilbert said that he and Cesar could not get along anymore. He said that it looked like there was a widening of misunderstanding between Cesar and himself.

And then Cesar said, "Well, Gilbert, you know how it is in this movement," and this and that, to try and convince Gilbert to stay. You see, Gilbert was one of the first guys who helped build the old NFWA. There was Cesar, Dolores Huerta, and Gilbert, they were the three originals. So you can imagine how shocked the others were when they heard Gilbert speak out like this. The other board members started pressuring Gilbert and me to withdraw our statements until Gilbert finally said, "O.K., I'll stay," after the others had put a lot of pressure on him. But then the board members turned to me and pounded me with anger, hitting me not with their fists but with their words.

Kent Winterrowd, who was a central executive administrator for the union, spoke up and said if I left the union that I would blast Cesar Chavez and tell people that the union is corrupt. He said that I had told him this in a conversation we had, although I had never said that to him. I had been talking to Kent before the meeting about the great centralization of power within the union and I said to him, "At the beginning it was needed, but as the union becomes more stabilized, I believe that the operations, the authority, and the power in the union should be decentralized to make it more democratic."

You can see that what I said to Kent kind of got twisted around in that meeting. It was very important that I make a distinction between the union and the union's leadership. This has been confused by a lot of people. My total support for the farmworkers has never changed. My disagreements and arguments have only been with the leadership, and you can see by the way Kent misinterpreted my statements that the leadership was very insecure about letting the general public know about some of its actions. I think it is best for the workers and the union supporters to know everything and then let them decide what is good and what is not good for the union. I want to be very clear about this. I was against my personal grievances being blown-up and used by outsiders who just wanted to hurt the union. But also I felt that an open debate of important and sometimes controversial issues was constructive for the growth of the union.

It was really becoming quite a struggle in that meeting. Everyone was kind of jumping on me and I was there by myself. Nobody took my side. Chris Hartmire was next to speak out against me. I should tell you something about Chris because even though he jumped on me too, at that meeting, he is one of the people in the union that I have the most respect for. Chris is a very intelligent person and he puts the principles of Christianity into action. As the Protestant minister who organized the Migrant Ministry, he has probably done more than any other church person to help support the unorganized farmworkers. I have often complained about some Christian leaders whose prejudices got in the way of Christian ethics, and they acted just like any other racist. But Chris was not that way. I admire Chris tremendously because he had been able to organize the different churches to really help the farmworkers. Although Chris was a Protestant and most of the farmworkers were Catholics, he wasn't bothered by the petty differences between the two religious groups and the feuds that had been going on for such a long time. Well, that's something special, and it took Chris Hartmire to bring them all together. Chris had no problem in getting along with Cesar, and it was Chris who was able to raise money when Cesar needed it in the beginning of the union. I have to be honest and give credit where it's due, and even if Chris defended Cesar, and Cesar maybe felt this way and that way about me, I wouldn't let it affect my feelings about Chris.

At the board meeting Chris stood up next and said, "But did you not say that you were going to write a book? Philip, why don't you just forget the idea of a book. I don't want to remember you as being against the union." I immediately saw what he was doing: attacking me by making up things because I had never talked to Chris or anybody about writing a book. I had not even thought of the idea myself. Perhaps Chris said that because of the critical statements made about the union by past Filipino leaders in the UFW after they quit the union. I also felt that Chris was saying these things just to defend Cesar. Well, Cesar can defend himself if he needs to. You see, when an individual is built up too much and made to seem like God, then you start defending him when you shouldn't. And you start confusing that person with the union. One person is not a union. Cesar is an important part of the union and has made tremendous contributions but he isn't the whole union. The farmworkers are the union. If you differ in opinion with Cesar, that doesn't mean you are attacking the union. But the board members have gotten this all confused.

So I said to Chris, "Even if I were to write a book, do you think I have spent all these years with the union just to attack it? I might have said to you once that something more honest about the union should be written. Besides, I'm not a journalist. You know I can't write a book. I was not trained to do that. I didn't have a chance to go to school and learn how to be a good writer. And I'm too old now even if I could do it."

Mark Grossman, Cesar's executive secretary, was also at that meeting and he said, "When I was attending the University of California at Irvine, you were writing articles and they were good."[9] I didn't say anything because I didn't feel it was worth responding to. I might have been able to put together a few short articles, but to write a book was something else. Writing a few short articles doesn't prove you can write a book. But somebody then said, "Yeah, but you can get some people to write it for you." And I said, "Sure, that's true. I could do that." You can see how afraid they were. I don't remember anyone on the board ever questioning Cesar when all those books were written about him.

Then Eliseo Medina—a Mexican who became second vice-president after my resignation and replaced me on the executive board—showed me a statement the officers of the union sign when they take the oath of office. It stated that after an officer resigns or retires, he should give back all his union-related papers to the union. I guess they were all thinking about Nixon and Watergate. But you see, these people were getting all mixed-up. The union wants to keep that stuff as historical documents so it won't get lost, but not to hide it from the public. Besides, all the papers I have except for a few notes I took, have duplicates in the union office, anyway. I thought it was a crazy thing for Eliseo to tell me. I said, "If you want my papers, you can come and get them tomorrow or right now. In fact, I'll go over to the office and get you all the papers right now." They were stuck then and didn't know what to say. Then I said, "If I write something I don't need those damn papers. I can go to the library and get books about the union and look up dates and how to spell names. That's the only information in those papers—that's all I would need." Then I think it was Chris who said, "For the book, though Philip, even if you don't get the papers, it's all in your head." He was still worried about me writing a book. Now, that was a more accurate statement. You see, I don't need those damn papers if I'm going to write a book. But what did he want me to do, turn in my head?!

Cesar spoke next and he said, "Well, Kent said this and Philip said that, so some goddamn guy must be lying." You know, Cesar is sometimes kind of intimidating. But he cannot scare me. I know how much he can do and I know what he can't do. He does not own me. I wanted to show him that nobody owned me there, you see, because I didn't want them to intimidate people. I don't think that's the right way to build a union. Then Cesar said to Jerry Cohen, the general counsel of the union, "Jerry, I think we should have a paper prepared to be signed here so that nothing will come out of this meeting, so nothing will be made public." Then Cesar went on, "What do you think, Jerry?" And Jerry just said, "O.K." I was a little surprised Jerry said that because he usually gives Cesar good advice. Jerry is a very good lawyer who has committed himself to the farmworkers struggle. In his own way Jerry is one of the few who speaks up against Cesar. Sometimes Cesar will suggest something and Jerry, as the general counsel, will state the facts, the laws, and then say to Cesar, "That's it, you know. I would not advise for you to do this." But then of course he leaves the final decision to Cesar and the board. Now Cesar, wanting to do the right thing, the smart thing, is not going to go against Jerry's advice because Jerry is a truthful and knowledgeable lawyer. If Cesar goes against Jerry, well, Jerry could say, "What the hell! I give you the facts and then you decide foolishly. What can I do then?" So Cesar has to show him some respect. After Jerry said O.K., they worked up this paper and everybody signed it after we took a short recess. Then they showed it to me when we reconvened and I said, "I'm not going to sign that shit. I want to preserve my own rights. I want my right to self-expression, my freedom of speech." Jerry tried very hard to get me to sign that paper. He said to me, "Remember, Philip, when you got sick in San Francisco and we asked Cesar to help you. We said a word for you at the hospital and helped you get admitted there."

I did get sick in San Francisco. I was having trouble with my prostate gland and I couldn't urinate. But Jerry in that meeting was trying to make it seem as if only because of Cesar I was admitted to the hospital and the union took care of my bill. He wanted me to feel that I owed it to Cesar and so, therefore, I should sign that damn paper. Well, all I said to Jerry was, "Yeah, I was in the hospital, I was sick. I remember that." The only trouble with Jerry's statement was that it wasn't true that, because of Cesar, I got admitted to the hospital, and that the union paid for my bill. Jerry didn't know it but Cesar did. I didn't want to embarrass Cesar at that meeting so I didn't say anything there. See, that's the way I am. Maybe I should have spoken up but I didn't. I felt it was Cesar's place and not mine to explain to Jerry what really happened. Sometimes I feel that silence, when you know the truth and your opponent does too, can be very powerful.

What really happened was that the union never paid my bill. When I got out of the hospital my bill was approaching $3,000, and the person in the union who really helped me was Ann McGregor, not Cesar. Ann was working for the Union Service Center then. This center is legally separated from the union, but we saw it as the same because its purpose was to help out the union members here and there when they needed it. Ann knew of this guy who lived in Richgrove near me and had worked for the Social Security department in Bakersfield. Ann gave me the address to his house and I went over to talk to him. You know, I can't even remember his name now, but he was very helpful because he had worked in the area of hospital benefits when he was with the Social Security department. At that time I had not yet been getting my retirement benefits because I had not applied for my Social Security. But because of my age I was already overdue. So that fellow arranged for my Social Security to pay for most of the hospital bill. However, there was still over $300 left that was not covered. I had Saint Mary's Hospital in San Francisco send the bill to Leroy Chatfield at the Union Service Center in La Paz. Leroy was in charge of the center then. But you know what? He just sent it back to me and said I had to pay it myself.

I told Cesar about this a long time ago—that I had to pay the bill myself because the center forwarded it to me and wouldn't pay it. Cesar said the union should have paid for it, but by then it was too late. Maybe Cesar really did want the union to pay. I don't know. But the fact is, I paid that bill because the union wouldn't. Yet I know that when the other officers had medical expenses they were always paid for by the union with no questions asked.

Well, Jerry kept trying to get me to sign that paper. He made it sound like I should sign because Cesar had been good to me. He was being very tactful at that meeting so he didn't exactly say it that way; he was beating around the bush, but that was his meaning. I still have respect for Cesar for many good things he has done for the farmworkers, but I don't owe him anything, and I had no obligations to him, especially to sign that piece of paper.

After a while the board took another recess. I was left there by myself in the room as everybody went out. I could see them through the windows talking to Pete Velasco outside. Pete is the third vice-president, the only other Filipino who was left on the board besides me. Pete's a nice guy but he just went along, always doing what he was told to do, and never trying to defend me. Pete was overprotective of his position as a board member and he didn't give a damn about me at that meeting. Pete and everyone else had already signed the prepared statement but I refused. So I was deserted.

Jerry came back in and again tried to convince me to sign that paper. This time I said, "Well Jerry, you are the general counsel of this union, but you know, I'm a part of this board too. Now I want to tell you again that I won't sign that paper because I want my freedom of speech to be preserved." I kept getting pressured by Jerry and finally I said to him that I would sign it, but only if I was guaranteed that my freedom of speech remained. Then I asked Jerry to show me that paper and someone took it out from a folder. At that time Cesar walked towards us, and soon he was standing in front of Jerry and me. Jerry said, "Let me see it again." He took the paper, re-read it hurriedly and said, "Well, it looks too broad. We'll fix it and then tomorrow we'll show it to you, Philip, O.K.?" I replied, "O.K."

Pete came back in and came over to me and said, "Well, you know, Philip, Marshall is kind of concerned about your health and he thinks that maybe you should go home for a while to rest." This meeting was at La Paz and since I don't have a place there of my own, I was staying at Pete's house. I guess Marshall meant that I should go rest at Pete's place there in La Paz. So I said, "O.K." again. I thought everyone was going to take a break since the meeting had gotten sort of hot and long. Pete and I stood up and walked out. I saw Richard Chavez and Dolores just standing there looking at me. Everyone was looking at me when we left the room on our way out. I looked around. All the people were still there and they didn't show any sign of leaving and I told Pete, "You know, Pete, they will have a meeting. People are not leaving." And Pete said, "Well, maybe, I guess so." So it was obvious they were just trying to get me out of that meeting. We went to Pete's house and Pete didn't even go back. That was the last board meeting I ever attended in La Paz.

Early the next morning Pete and I went back for the rest of the meeting but there wasn't anyone there, and we were told the meeting had finished the day before. So, I never did sign that damn paper. I have seen Jerry since then but he's never mentioned it again to me. I think Jerry realized that if he pushed me to sign it, he could be involved in some kind of conflict of interest because I had told him at the meeting that it was a violation of my rights and he was the one who was trying to get me to sign it. He was my lawyer too and was supposed to give me good advice. The way I see it, he was pushing himself into a conflict with his oath as a lawyer, and if I had gone to court, I would have explained this to the judge. I think Jerry would then have been in trouble. So that was the end of that.

So it was at that meeting in La Paz that I told the board that I was officially leaving the union. I didn't say I was going to retire. They used that term "retire" to make it sound like I had been willing and I was not forced out. They wanted the public to hear the word "retire." I wanted everyone to understand that I didn't retire. I left the union, because the way I saw it, it was the board's actions over the years, over the last 12 years, that forced me to leave, and they just didn't want to admit it.

There is one last controversial issue, a very important one, and again, I was the only dissenting vote on the board. This issue came up at the last couple of meetings, and for me, it was like the final blow. Cesar was invited to visit the Philippines by Marcos. Cesar introduced the subject before the board by saying that he had been talking to Andy Imutan and Andy told him over the phone that Marcos was extending an invitation to Cesar to visit the Philippines. Andy was acting as a middleman between Marcos and Cesar. Andy used to be with the union. He was one of the original board members. After Larry Itliong, Andy was the most important Filipino leader in the union. Along with his wife Luming, they proved themselves one of the top boycott organizers in Boston, Maryland, and New York City back in the late 1960s. But Andy left the UFW later, even after Larry. He told me that just like Larry he felt the Filipinos didn't have any power in the union because the leadership didn't care about Filipinos. So Andy went off on his own and started some service organization in Stockton to provide social services for Filipino farmworkers. It was called the Bayanihan. He got over $600,000 just from the State Manpower Agency alone for his project. But Andy has gotten into a lot of trouble because Bayanihan gets federal and state money. Yet, Andy apparently used the center to promote a lot of Marcos propaganda here in California. It looks like Andy is sort of Marcos' man here in the valley. When you get federal and state funds, you are not supposed to take political sides, especially for a foreign government. People who have been to Andy's office tell me that he has a picture of Marcos right there on the wall. Well, you can see that Andy's politics have gotten all mixed-up. He says he's trying to help Filipino farm-workers in the U.S., and then he supports a Philippine dictator who puts farmworkers in jail for organizing activities.

Cesar wanted to know the reaction of the board to this invitation. He was interested to see if the board would approve it or not. Jim Drake was the first to say something. I heard Jim mutter in barely an audible voice that the trip would be good for the Filipino farmworkers. That's all he said. He was referring to the fact that Cesar had told the Filipinos a long time ago, before Marcos declared martial law in the Philippines, that he would visit their country someday. Cesar had done lots of special things for the Mexicans and he had visited Mexico. So he thought if he went to the Philippines it would show the Filipino farmworkers that he really cared about them. Then Marshall gave a little approving comment. Those were the only two I heard make favorable comments at the time. Chris Hartmire spoke next and he gave a different opinion. He said, "What are you going to talk about over there, the UFW? They don't have free unions there, you know." You could see that after Chris said this Cesar and the others didn't want to talk too much more about it. But then Cesar turned to me and asked, "Well, Philip, what do you think?" And I said, "No, I don't approve of it. I don't like the form of government Marcos has created because it's very oppressive. It's a dictatorship. There are thousands of political prisoners, people are arrested without charges or benefit of trial." I told them that the United Nations, Amnesty International, and some international legal organization, like the International Commission of Jurists, and even the U.S. State Department, have documented widespread use of torture. Then I quoted the wage of 14 cents to 18 cents an hour over there and said that Marcos had declared labor unions illegal. He had prohibited all strikes in the Philippines (Presidential Decree No. 823) and had arrested all labor leaders. Two of the most prominent labor leaders, attorney Herman C. Lagnam and Victor Reyes, were arrested by the military and they have not been heard from since. But that's all I said. I could see that after Chris and I spoke, Cesar wasn't in the mood to listen anymore. I know how he gets. It doesn't do any good if I kept talking so I just shut up. Then Cesar said, "Well, all right." And he moved on right away to the next order of business and that's all that was said about that issue. He didn't want to decide then because he could see that his position was weak.

Well, Cesar took that trip anyway just before the UFW convention on August 26 to 28, 1977. He was accompanied by his brother Richard, and Andy Imutan. I have no proof that the board ever took a vote whether Cesar should go or not. They may have voted on it without me after I went to Pete's house to rest at my last board meeting in La Paz. If they voted on it, then it's really ironic because Pete and I were the only Filipinos on the board then and neither of us was there to cast our votes. But maybe they didn't even take a vote. Maybe Cesar just decided it by himself.

Cesar later told me that the majority of the board was for his trip to the Philippines, and he also told me that I was the only one who disapproved of it. Even Chris Hartmire who spoke out against the trip at the board meeting was supporting Cesar's trip later on in a community meeting at the Delano High School auditorium where Cesar was asked to explain and defend his trip to the Philippines. I can tell you now, that of all the decisions Cesar has made in his career, this one to visit the Philippines as a guest of Marcos may prove to be the most controversial. You would think that Cesar was smart enough not to have been tricked by Marcos and Andy. But Cesar played right into Marcos' hand. It was tremendously good publicity for Marcos and the pro-Marcos people like Andy here in the States, and nothing but bad publicity for Cesar. Cesar had his picture taken with Marcos, and Marcos gave him a special Presidential Appreciation Award! Cesar was even quoted as saying that from what he had seen it looked like Marcos' martial law was really helping the people. What Cesar did there in the Philippines was the saddest day in the history of the farmworkers movement in this country. It was just a disgrace. Cesar was toasting with Marcos and all those phony farm and labor leaders appointed by Marcos at the presidential palace, and at the same time, on the other side of Manila, the real union leaders and farmworkers were in jail. Some of them have been in jail since the first day of martial law—that's over five years now. And many have been tortured in the most terrible ways you can imagine. I have to say now what I feel in my heart. I cannot hold it back any longer.

Just before the last UFW convention I attended, I received a notice that I had to be at the convention a day earlier to attend a special meeting of the board which was supposed to meet at the convention center. At that meeting Cesar was telling us what we had to do during the convention. It was then he told us that the Consul General of the Philippines would be the guest speaker on the first day of the convention. Cesar also told us that on the second day of the convention, the secretary of labor from the Philippines, Blas Ople, would be another guest speaker. Then he said that we had to endorse Andy's organization, Bayanihan, and that Andy would be there at the convention, too, with his wife, Luming, as special guests. Cesar never before brought any of this up to the board. He never asked for my opinion on this. He just told us at that special meeting that's the way it will be.

These conventions are orchestrated to give the union members a certain impression. Everything is planned ahead of time, but when you are there, and if you don't know what's going on, you think that things just happen on their own spontaneously. It was obvious that Cesar was making a big push to impress the Filipinos at this convention, but in my opinion, it was all show. There was no real substance of Filipino rank-and-file support for what Cesar was doing. The only Filipinos he was impressing besides Andy were those from the Philippines, the Marcos supporters.

When the Philippine Consul General got up to speak on the first day of the convention, Cesar arranged for all the *manongs* living at Agbayani Village to escort the guest to the stage. Pete joined the escort too because Cesar asked him to. But Cesar didn't ask me because he knew I'd refuse. The *manongs*, except a few, didn't really know what was going on. They just thought it was some kind of an honor for them. They didn't really understand all the politics involved. I think Andy and some others told the *manongs* that before martial law, the Philippines was a mess. But now there is no more corruption, no more pickpockets, and the streets are clean and that everyone loves Marcos. You know, typical propaganda like that. Well, these old-timers who hadn't been back to the Philippines in a long time hadn't read any of the special reports exposing the corrupt practices and dictatorial policies of Marcos. So of course they just believed all the propaganda. What the old-timers believe is really their own business, if they want to believe all that shit I can't do anything about that. But what I don't like to see is how Cesar and the representatives of the Marcos government used these old-time Filipinos, who have been laboring here in this country for over 50 years with no rewards to show for their hard work, to help promote their own political ambitions. And the same procedure took place the next day by having Pete and the *manongs* escort Ople, the Secretary of Labor, when he spoke. You could see how well it was all orchestrated.

The people in the audience applauded politely for both speakers but that was all. The general rank and file was a bit shocked by these guests. I heard later that many people didn't want to applaud or stand up when these guys were introduced. There was only one person, however, who actually voiced a verbal protest and that was during Cesar's introductory speech for Ople. She is a lawyer who was before a legal advisor for the union. The young attorney was Deborah A. Vollmer. She called out, "*Abajo con martial law*! Down with martial law in the Philippines! Down with the Marcos dictatorship!" After she said that security guards came up to her and told her that there was a message for her out at the front door. She was suspicious and said, "I don't believe you. You just want to put me out." And they said, "No, there really is a message for you." When she went to the front door they grabbed her official pass and threw her out bodily and wouldn't let her back in.

When the Philippine officials spoke, the subject was always the glorification of Marcos and his new society and the new freedom and dignity of the workers which, of course, was their government propaganda. The consul general talked about U.S. democracy in this society and how

Marcos is trying to achieve a new kind of Filipino democracy through martial law. He was saying all sorts of contradictory things like that, comparing martial law with democracy.

Well, here's a real interesting thing. After Ople spoke on the second day of the convention, Rudy Reyes stood up and went to the microphone. Rudy's a Filipino who used to be in Delano but now is down in Coachella. In fact, I think he's helping in the union office down there. Rudy said into the microphone, "Well, I would like to thank the Consul General and the Secretary of Labor for their speeches. But when the Secretary of Labor gets back to the Philippines, I hope he does not forget to tell Marcos to lift martial law." And the people right away stood up and clapped their hands and cheered and finally were able to show their true feelings. Rudy's remarks got a large and loud reception. None of the UFW officials on stage clapped their hands but I stood up and clapped my hands because I wanted to show how I felt. Then Ople looked at Cesar and said, "I would like to answer that." And Cesar said, "Yeah, go ahead." And so Ople said a few more things but I can't remember now what he said. When he got through speaking, I stood up and went to Cesar. I wanted to have the microphone because I too had something to say. But Cesar said to me, "What are you going to say?" And I said, "It's coming from me." I was pointing to my heart and I didn't feel like I had to tell Cesar the exact words I was going to use. Cesar didn't ask Ople what he was going to say when Ople wanted to reply to Rudy's statements. Cesar then said to me, "No, because you're going to insult him (Ople)." That is exactly what Cesar said to me then. So, what could I do? I went back to my seat. But everyone at the convention saw my exchange with Cesar. You can see what a sad state of affairs Cesar had come to when he was officially gagging a union officer who had been with the union since its inception while allowing a representative of a right-wing foreign government a free voice to speak to the union rank and file.

Next, the business part of the convention followed when they elected new officers. This of course was all planned-out ahead like everything else. The officers elected are those chosen by Cesar ahead of time unless there is a strong move within the rank and file to oppose the candidate of Cesar's choice. But I don't think that could happen in the UFW because Cesar was and still is much too powerful. So the nomination and election was just a matter of procedure. In appearance it is very democratic but behind that appearance is a slate that is already decided. Cesar will be president, Dolores will be first vice-president, and so on. You could see at this convention how well-planned out everything was because it was Fred Abad, a Filipino, who nominated Cesar to continue as president of the UFW. Before, at the past convention, they didn't ask a Filipino to nominate Cesar. But it all went together at this convention — Cesar's trip to the Philippines, having these Philippine government officials as guest speakers, and having a Filipino nominate Cesar. So Fred Abad nominated Cesar and then a seconding nomination followed, and then they had to get enough votes to qualify the candidate. Of course they ask if there are any other nominations but there wasn't another candidate besides Cesar, so that's that. And here comes the motion to have a vote of acclamation that Cesar will be elected unanimously. Well, the same procedure followed for Dolores Huerta for first vice-president.

When they came to my position for second vice-president, somebody stood up and nominated Eliseo Medina. He's a Mexican and he was Cesar's choice to replace me. This had been decided ahead of time. Well, some of the Filipinos were kind of surprised because I was the second vice-president and had held that position officially since the UFW's first convention, but nobody stood up to nominate me. It had not yet been announced to the audience that I was leaving the union. So one Filipino who didn't know about my plans, Ernie Barrientos, went to the microphone and nominated me. I stood up right away and started to go to the microphone. I wanted to tell the people there that I wasn't a candidate anymore and that I was leaving the union so they wouldn't get confused or disappointed by the way the proceedings were taking place. But when I stood up, Erwin DeShetler called to me and said, "Philip, sit down and wait to speak. You'll get your turn." DeShetler is an old guy who is the retired president of the Glass Blowers Union and he was sitting up there on the stage behind the officers with the other special guests of the union. We are good friends and have always talked very confidentially. I think he's a very nice guy. Since I had been so close to him, I listened to his advice and sat down. Then Cesar said, "Is there a second for Brother Philip?" Everyone was looking at everyone else but there was none. Since there was no second I was not qualified to be a candidate. Then Cesar looked at me and said, "You have anything to say?" I said, "Yes," of course. I suppose DeShetler had stopped me the first time because of procedure. This time I stood up and went to the microphone right away because I didn't want to miss the opportunity to speak. There had been many occasions in the past when Cesar didn't want me to speak and now he was saying it was O.K., so I took it without hesitation.

As soon as I stood up and walked to the microphone you should have seen the reaction of the people. They really applauded. They gave me a big reception and I raised my hand to acknowledge it. I felt it in my heart and I was very grateful for it. Well, first I told them that I was getting out of the union and I made it clear that I was resigning and not retiring. Then I spoke about my feelings about the farmworkers movement and some of the problems that result when you don't allow freedom of expression within the union. See, I wasn't going to talk to the people at that convention about all the differences between me and Cesar but I thought they should understand some of the general problems that I have seen and that led to my frustrations in the union. I said we should try to make a distinction between the farmworkers movement and the leadership during different periods of the movement. I explained that my support for the farmworkers and their movement had never changed just because I had disagreed with the leadership. I told the people that a diversification of ideas should not be seen as being against the union. In fact, this should be seen as a strength of the union. I told them that it is natural for lots of ideas to be expressed in a union like ours because a movement survives by attracting lots of different people to it. That's the only way it can guarantee its growth. All these different ideas enrich the union but only if the leadership was broad-minded enough to accept different new ideas.

I told the convention members that I thought that the leadership of the union today had become reactionary. This might have sounded terrible to say but I believe it's really true. In my speech I said, "I cannot understand why a resolution was passed to condemn the dictatorship of Nicaragua and at the same convention, to praise the dictatorship of the Philippines." I said that I didn't believe the speeches made by the consul general and secretary of labor of the Philippines. I said I didn't believe that they had tried to make democracy work through martial law. How the hell can you put together these two opposite things? I said, "You know, brothers and sisters, it cannot be hot and cold at the same time. So therefore, they must not know what they are talking about." You see, the secretary of labor said that through martial law they were trying to keep democracy in the Philippines for freedom, equality, justice, and the dignity of man. Well, how the hell could that be when the political prisoners are being tortured there in the Philippines without charges and without trial? Then I hit martial law real hard because I had to. All the contradictions of Cesar's actions over the past few weeks and months were actions that I felt were a slap in the face to our farmworkers struggle. These feelings I had were all in my heart and I couldn't keep them inside any longer. I felt thankful to the audience for their tremendous approval of what I was saying. My speech gave them an opportunity to express their true feelings. You could also see that the response to my speech kind of silenced the other board members. Before this I had only spoken my opinions at the board meetings. I rarely said anything in public that differed from the board's opinion in all my years with the union and never with such vigor as I did at the convention.

After my speech they followed the same procedure to elect Medina as second vice-president, and like the others, he was voted in by acclamation. I was still sitting up there on the stage and Arguelles was sitting near me and I told that guy, "Why don't you give me some materials because I want to know exactly what the hell is going on there in the Philippines." And he said, "Well, sure. I'll send them to you." Well, he never sent me anything.

∽

I have thought about it a lot but I really don't know why Cesar decided to make that trip to the Philippines. I can just guess like everyone else. Cesar says it was to bring the Filipinos closer to the union but that doesn't make any sense. If you are going to be realistic and truthful then you have to admit that the Filipinos are leaving the farm labor force. The Filipinos who were important in the farm labor movement at one time are now dying out. They belong to my generation. The young Filipinos are finding better opportunities in other areas. Just a few months ago I met some Filipino nurses in Visalia who used to pick grapes here in Delano when they were younger, perhaps while going to school, and now they work in hospitals. And old-timers around here who are still picking grapes, their kids go to college and are seeking better opportunities. Every year there will be fewer jobs in the farms because of mechanization, and the bulk of new farmworkers will be coming from the Mexican population.

Another reason Cesar gave for his trip was to see how Marcos' land reform program was doing. Cesar got over there and was told this and that by Marcos' men. Then, just like that, before the press, Cesar praised the program the way it was told to him and showed to him by Marcos' publicity officers. He never did any private or personal investigation on his own because if he had he would have known that the actual amount of land titles being transferred to farmers is minute in number. According to a study done by the World Council of Churches, only 2 or 3 percent of all the agricultural land in the Philippines, first of all, are covered under Marcos' land reform program, and of this, only a very small percentage of tenant farmers qualify to purchase land. On the other hand, there are still giant American corporations like Del Monte and Dole who own thousands of acres in the Philippines. These two companies moved from Hawaii because in the Philippines Marcos made it illegal for the workers to strike or organize their own unions which, in effect, means that wages will be kept low. And naturally, these giant U.S. agribusinesses are exempt from any land reform. But damn it, is Cesar too dumb to see that these U.S. agribusinesses in the Philippines are connected with their counterparts here in California, through the same economic system that exploits U.S. farmworkers for bigger profits? That these are the same agribusinesses we in the farmworkers movement have been fighting against for so many years? Cesar's trip to the Philippines and having Marcos' government officials speak at the convention contradict everything Cesar has been fighting for all these years. It contradicts the struggle of the farmworkers movement. I know that Cesar was given bad advice by some Filipinos like Andy, and unfortunately, Cesar fell for it. So maybe you can say that Cesar made an honest mistake. Maybe he thought he was doing the right thing. But if he made an honest mistake then he could admit it. But Cesar didn't admit that he made any mistake.

After that trip many of the union's supporters, especially the churches, wanted to talk to Cesar in private in La Paz. Their intention was to give Cesar the facts about what was happening in the Philippines because it was obvious that Cesar had fallen for Marcos's propaganda through Andy. These supporters were very disappointed about Cesar's trip and the statement he made to the press in praise of the Marcos martial law government. They wanted Cesar to recognize that he made a mistake in going to the Philippines because what Marcos stands for is in direct contrast to the ideals Cesar has been fighting for in the farmworkers movement. They just wanted Cesar to retract many of the things he had said in praise of Marcos. The union supporters were being very fair and considerate of Cesar. They all had a tremendous amount of respect for him. They knew that Cesar had unselfishly done more for the farmworkers than any other person since the Delano strike and, in fact, if it wasn't for Cesar Chavez, perhaps the farmworkers movement might not be as successful as it is today. They were trying to give Cesar an opportunity in a private meeting to retract the things he had said over there in the Philippines. They were trying to keep the door open, but Cesar closed it. Instead of holding a private meeting in La Paz, Cesar changed it to a public meeting in Delano. He said in his opening remarks at that meeting that he didn't come to apologize but only to clarify his position in relation to martial law in the Philippines. And when people in the audience asked Cesar questions like "Do you support Marcos's martial law?," Cesar wouldn't answer. He had officials of the Philippine government who were there answer for him. The union supporters who were there and especially the church people were not very happy with Cesar and lost their trust in him that day.

Outside the meeting a group of union supporters were marching in a circle, protesting Cesar's involvement with martial law in the Philippines. They were walking around, chanting slogans, and expressing their displeasure with Cesar's actions. There were church people there, ministers, priests, lay, some students, really a mixed group. A couple of the people who were in the group were radical young Filipinos who associated themselves with the Communist Party. They may not have been actual party members, I don't know, but everyone knew they were sympathetic to the idea. That mixed group was walking around and chanting their protests when Dolores Huerta came out of the meeting and started verbally attacking the young radical Filipinos out of the blue. She shouted at them, "You like Cuba so much why don't you go there?" Dolores' remarks were totally uncalled for and had nothing to do with the events that were taking place. This wasn't the first time Dolores, or Cesar for the matter, had used red-baiting tactics to attack or humiliate someone who opposed them. But for me I had already decided to disassociate myself from this kind of attitude.

Some people have said that Cesar made that trip for money for himself or at least money for the union which was always in bad financial straits. I have heard that Marcos is the kind of guy who uses money to garner support for his martial law regime. But Cesar has never been that kind of a person. Cesar has never taken money for anything. Since there was no apparent reason at the time why Cesar would act this way, people were grabbing for any explanation they thought made sense.

I liked Cesar and even with all our differences I trusted him and I defended him publicly for 12 years. In 1970 I wrote an article for *The Catholic Worker* about the union and the last paragraph was written in praise of Cesar. In it I wrote: "I believe we have the right brother with a greater sense of judgement and proportion than anyone of us. He has a strong mind to compensate for a painful back. He is known to be color-blind while leading a farmworkers union consisting of a rainbow of races.

We will always need such an honest, compassionate and fearless leader. His name is Cesar Chavez."[10] When I wrote that I was being very sincere. But times do change and even at my age I can learn new things, and now, in the end it is all reversed. The trust is gone.

Since I left the union it's kind of funny or ironic but I feel liberated. I feel that now I have more freedom. I know that even in this country as a minority my freedom is limited, but in the union, it was like I was in jail. That's the way I was feeling in the end. I could not do or say certain things. Sometimes I said things that were against the union but then I would feel guilty. So, as soon as I left I felt so liberated. I could say what I felt in my heart and nobody could censure me.

"My continual struggle"

I stayed with the union for 12 years because for me the struggle of the workers in this country is the most important struggle. Our system in this country continually tries to play the workers off against each other when of course the workers' struggle is really against the big corporations. And here I'm talking about the problem of the profits of the owners versus the wages and other benefits of the workers. It's crucial that the minorities who live in this country understand the rules of the system, the capitalist rules. This system can be very dangerous and confusing if you don't understand how it works. It is not accidental that this system completely fails to supply jobs for everyone. The system needs unemployed people as sort of a reminder to those who are working that they'd better be good and not complain too much. This system also intentionally allows an increasing number of workers to enter the country and then gets these new immigrants, the unemployed, and the other workers to fight among themselves for the jobs.

New immigrants, who will compete with the workers already here, are arriving everyday from the Philippines, Puerto Rico, the Arab countries, from Jamaica, and especially Mexico. Third World countries have been exploited so much by the multinational corporations that their people, moved by extreme poverty, leave their home countries to seek work in an industrialized country like the United States. The multinationals suck the wealth out of their homeland like a vampire sucks blood. And these same big businesses here greet these new immigrants with open arms. These poor foreigners bring their cheap labor which means increasing profits for the big corporations. When the present group of workers here start to get organized and win some of their struggles for better wages and benefits, then the big agribusinesses here in California, with the help of the government, try to bring in new groups of workers.

All you have to do is look at the history of farm labor here in California to see this happening. The growers have always tried to get the different groups of workers—the Chinese, the Japanese, the Filipino and the Mexicans—to fight among themselves for the jobs. And don't forget that the large influx of new immigrant laborers also serves as a safety valve against the outbreak of revolution in smaller Third World countries by continually draining their manpower and helping, if only a little, to ease the Third World countries' massive unemployment.

This issue of workers coming from other countries was always a controversial one in the union too, because many of the farmworkers, especially from Mexico, were undocumented workers. I always took an opposing view to Cesar's position on the undocumented workers. I think it's because I am more of an internationalist than Cesar. In fact, I am the only board member who raised objections to the union's policy against the undocumented worker. From the beginning of the union Cesar had been very insistent that undocumented workers should not be in this country and because Cesar felt this way the union has never supported the rights of the undocumented workers.

Well, the way I see it, it is not a question of whether they should be here or not. The fact is they are here. For me workers are workers no matter where they come from or whatever reasons they are here. And as a union we have to protect their rights. It is the job of the labor movement to unite all workers regardless of their color, nationality, language, or whatever. We can't let the growers and the government trick us into playing their game of dividing workers up into different competing groups. That only creates rivalries between the workers.

I view the farmworkers movement as multiracial, multinational. History tells us that farmworkers of every race and nationality have been involved in building this movement and farmworkers of all nationalities were immigrants at one time, some undocumented when they first came to this country. If we don't fight for the rights of all workers then the growers and the government will continue to use them against us like they have so often done in the past.

Others argue that the undocumented worker takes away jobs here in this country. Well, it only seems that they are taking away jobs, but actually, it's only because there are not enough jobs provided by the economy. It's the government's job to help people get work. It's the government, anyway, that really allows minority workers to continuously come into this country. The government continues to let new workers enter the U.S., and at the same time, does very little to increase the number of jobs available because the government is run by agents and representatives of big business.

If you live here, of course, you have to go along with the system but that doesn't mean you can't make some changes here and there to improve the balance. See, I'm a very radical fellow, but I know that sometimes you can only get positive changes slowly over a long period of time. The poor people and the working people have to keep struggling for more and better social legislation. I'm basically an optimistic person and I think the trend is going that way no matter what the big guys at the top say or think. They know it and that's why they give in now and then. They don't want to lose everything so they compromise. Workers, by fighting and struggling together, get a little more here, a little more there.

Even if you look at the Supreme Court back in the Warren years, you can see that some of its decisions were getting better. Even some of the conservative justices decided a little bit more for the poor people because the situation was changing all the time and the pressure was greater for those at the top to give up a little. You know, judges are always concerned about their achievements in history. I think they really care more about their own image in history than about the poor people. So, they make little changes here and there when the pressure from the workers and the poor increases. They also make some concessions because they are trying to save part of the capitalist system.

In this system companies insist on making huge profits. That's the only way they can see it. But many of these companies are so poorly run that they wouldn't make one penny if it wasn't for all the assistance they get from the government which too often acts as a partner to business. You know, the politicians call it socialism when they give a little money to the poor to keep them alive but when they give huge amounts of money to a big business to keep it alive they call it "subsidies."

Well, it's easy to see that the rich are just goddamn parasites whose only work is to count the money they have from the workers. But I think in the long run the system will change. It has to because as the corporations get bigger and expand all over the world, and the masses of workers become more and more the victims of unemployment and starvation wages, then the pressure from the bottom, from these workers, for some major changes has to increase.

I have seen many changes in the time I have been here. For one thing, the American middle class has progressed a lot since I first came to this country. Twenty years ago, nobody supported the farmworkers. Today, all you've got to say is, the farmworkers movement, and lots of people will help. It's still not easy and it's still only a minority but there has been tremendous change. Also, there are far more opportunities available for Filipinos today. Of the Filipinos like myself, who came to the U.S. before WWII, very few have succeeded to better their lives. A Filipino in the U.S. then, even though he was a college graduate would still be a dishwasher—that's all there was. I have friends who had degrees and they were working in hotels or with me in the restaurants. There was a guy I knew who had a degree in civil law and had even received his doctorate too, but he was just washing dishes and being a busboy with me in Chicago. But it's different for the college graduate now. Although their fathers, who may have had a college degree too, could be nothing better than a dishwasher, now the sons and daughters and the new Filipinos arriving have many more opportunities available to them.

Fifty years ago in the U.S. there were no Filipinos working in banks, no Filipinos teaching in schools. But now you find them teaching, working in the banks; they are architects, lawyers, and doctors. There have been many changes but still not enough. Although Filipinos have much better chances today, as an ethnic group compared to the rest of the population, they are still almost at the bottom. You still see very few Filipinos in positions with any real influence or power.

But as I tell young Filipinos, it's important to try to improve yourself, get a college education, learn a skill. Although things are a lot better today you've still got to prove to employers that you are qualified

148

and that you should be listened to. The Filipinos can learn a lot from observing other minority groups in this country who have made a place for themselves. When I was living in Chicago, I always worked for that Jewish guy, Weiskopf, and I learned many things just being around Jewish people. They are a real minority but they have become very developed intellectually. They hold high positions in government and business. I know there aren't enough Jewish votes to elect a Jewish senator but there are Jewish senators and that's because they have prepared themselves properly so people would listen to them and vote them into responsible positions.

I want the Filipinos to learn to be more responsible too, so that when they are in a position of power, they will be able to represent people fairly. It's not unusual to see a minority in an influential position only use that position to promote himself personally to the detriment often of other minorities. So what good does that do? I have learned through my experiences in this country that minorities do not have a monopoly on virtue and are just as likely to exploit as a white person when tempted by power and influence.

If Filipinos still want to support the UFW, well, that's fine, I wouldn't stop them. In fact, I would encourage them, but only if they prepare themselves properly to be an important part of the union. If they don't they will just be used and will get hurt like the Filipinos have in the past. You can't just be a farmworker anymore if you want to participate in the movement. The Filipinos who want to support the UFW should get a good education first and become experts in certain areas so the union will need their services. That's when they can support the movement and really play an important role. That's when the other people in the movement will ask for their opinion, and their opinion then will have some weight. If for whatever reason they do not stay with the union, then they can still get out and be doctors, lawyers, accountants, or whatever. But, what's important is that they will not be crucified because they're just an ignorant worker. I've seen Filipinos come and join the union, work for the union for years and years, and then because of some political disagreement, one that they usually didn't understand, they got kicked out of the union and had nothing to fall back on. All they could do was go back to the farm and work in the fields and often they were not even wanted there because they had been blacklisted by the growers due to their previous union activities.

Being a minority within a minority and without skill or profession, Filipinos have had no chance in the farmworkers movement. The leadership will only keep and use them as figureheads. One thing I have learned about the leadership of the union is that it can take advantage of you. It wants you to spend all your life there with the union, but then when you are in need, it doesn't really help you. I would be a damn liar and deceitful if I didn't tell the truth to my own people and others who care for the union. Lying to them would make them feel bitter towards the union. It's better for people to understand what they are getting into. Promises that can't be delivered are unfair and should not be made.

In fact, all farmworkers, Mexican as well as Filipino, should be aware of the fact that there will be fewer jobs on the farms in the future. Every year there is more mechanization of work in the fields. Farmworkers must prepare themselves for these changes.

Obviously it's hard for young Filipinos who don't have an education and are poor, and the only occupation they have is farm work. But if they get a chance to go to school I would encourage them to do that. They can support the union and still try to improve themselves. I just don't want somebody to devote himself or herself blindly to the union. I've seen some young Filipinos who were good students at universities—some were even close to graduation—who dropped out of school to devote themselves full-time to the political struggle. Well, this is foolishness. There has to be a compromise. That's one thing I have learned here and that's what I try to tell young Filipinos. I want them to prepare themselves. This might sound kind of conservative but it's for our survival and that's the most important thing. Education and knowledge are the power of the minorities in this society. It's a hard lesson to learn but one I want to give to the Filipino youth. Filipinos must let good reason guide them through hard times. The youth especially should not let themselves be used as radical fanatics just for the momentary satisfaction of illusionary goals. Sometimes young radicals criticize me for saying and thinking this way. They think this isn't a very revolutionary approach. But they don't realize that there is a difference between being a revolutionary in this country today than, let's say, in China 40 years ago or even Cuba 20 years ago. Anyway, people like Mao Tse-tung, Fidel Castro, and Che Guevara were all educated men. People listened to them and had a lot of respect for them.

Some young people think that dressing a certain way or wearing your hair a certain way or having a beard makes you a radical. Well, different dress styles perhaps can express progressive thinking but the progressive spirit has to be from within, not just in the way you dress or how you look externally. After all, shit, look at even the growers' sons today, right here in Delano. They got beards too. But their politics are far from being radical or progressive. Dress styles are always so relative to the times anyway. When I first came to the States, all students, even progressive ones or poor ones like myself, wore ties and had nice haircuts. We all looked like people who worked in banks, young professional types, like the rich students back in the Philippines.

Back in the 1960s, when I started going around the colleges to talk about the union, there were many colleges I couldn't speak at unless I had on the proper attire—tie and a sweater or something like that, with a haircut—because the audience would look me over from head to toe and prejudge my politics based on my appearance. A few years later in the late 1960s and 70s, I could go around making speeches for the union in this old jacket and didn't even have to worry about my shoes being clean or not. Then it was O.K. because some of the people in the audience were even barefooted themselves, even those who had Ph.D.s. The professors looked like students and the students were dressed-up like farmworkers, so what the hell! I finally felt at home. It took until I was 70 years old for the rest of the world's dress code to finally catch up with mine.

Perhaps my outlook of the radical movement is different from others. I try to be practical because I've been here a long time and I know how difficult it is to survive. If I had a chance, even today, I would go into business as long as I don't step on anybody else. I'd go into business to survive so I can feed myself, because looking at it realistically, nobody is going to feed me. I'm just sensible about this sort of thing. As I said before I own a piece of land and it gave me some security when I was still with the union. What I have is not much, just a little, but it's something for me, especially at my age to fall back on.

All in all I have faith in the younger generation. They are much more knowledgeable and progressive than my generation. I know that sometimes they are held back by their parents but they are looking around for a better way. It's a long process and I know it's very difficult for people to get together and win struggles. There are many hard lessons I have learned here in this country and the younger generation will learn them, too, and will do an even better job than we did.

When the Filipinos were drafted into the army in WWII, we were encouraged by the army to become U.S. citizens. But there was a great resistance among us to do so because our experiences in this country were very unpleasant and we actually felt hurt by the way we had been treated. What we had learned about this country from the little education we received back in the Philippines was very different from what we experienced when we got here. When I was asked to become a citizen I rejected the opportunity. It was only after the war when I seriously realized that this was really becoming my home and that if I wanted to stay here I had better start exercising my rights. I got my citizenship not because I embraced the capitalist system but more because of my belief in a working democracy. I wanted to have the right to vote so I could start expressing myself politically. I also wanted to be able to buy property and have security and protect myself against some reactionary politician who on a whim would pass some legislation that could get a non-citizen kicked out of the country. That's when I started to realize and understand for the first time that it was not only Filipinos who suffered from racial discrimination and prejudice in this country but all poor people. I realized that I couldn't even start to struggle against these injustices without the rights and individual power that went along with citizenship. So, for my generation, taking our citizenship was part of our road to survival.

I see life as a continuous progressive struggle—a group of people struggle to survive. They get older and then they are gone. But the next ones will come together and solve some of their problems. They'll align themselves with others and make advances that the previous generation wasn't able to accomplish.

And in this struggle to improve ourselves I have come to the conclusion that the good leaders are the ones who have a good understanding of where the people's political consciousness is at. The good leaders also have a good appreciation of time. See, you can be radical but it's no good unless you are radical at the right time and in a realistic sense. Maybe you can try to speed things up a little, but you can't go way ahead of the people or else you'll lose them. There are many different reasons why people will resist change and you've got to understand this. Sometimes people resist because they really don't understand the issues—often they are confused and do the opposite of what they really should do. Lots of times they resist because of things they have at stake: they have jobs, friends, and maybe they have some property or some kind of business, you know. So, while some of the people are going one way, others are pulling back the other way. Great leaders are the ones who can correctly judge the mood of the people.

I've learned in the farmworkers movement that the most essential thing is the people: they need to be taught and given good honest leadership, but most important of all, a leader has to know what they are ready for and what they are not ready for.

Young radicals often get too impatient and struggle for change without the full support of the workers. This is a big mistake that many well-intentioned progressive people have made. See, it is essential that progressive people work with the labor unions. The success of any positive changes in this country depends on the strength of the workers and the organizations that hold the workers together are the unions. Many radicals have abandoned the workers because they see that the big unions have become conservative and dominated by corrupt officials. And the radicals see the workers as a conservative, even reactionary, element. Some of these criticisms are very true, but still, you should never desert the workers. Fight to improve the unions and educate the workers. Nothing will really change in this country without the total support of the working class. And of course, the workers have to continue their struggle to improve their unions and make them truly democratic institutions.

$\sim$

People have said to me at different times, "Why don't you go back to where you came from." When I first came to this country I didn't understand why people would say this to me, and boy, I wanted to cry. People even said that to me many years later even when they knew I was a citizen of this country. I always felt so sad and hurt when that happened.

My public school education in the Philippines and over here didn't teach me why people would act that way. But through my political education in the union and my own reading I now understand. People become insecure and afraid in this country, and our economic system turns them against each other and they learn to hate. This happens when people don't understand this system they live in, they get confused, and they fight each other, but really, you know, they should fight the system that teaches them to think this way.

In my way of thinking the U.S. is my country, and so is the Philippines. I believe that people should be able to choose wherever they want to be and I don't agree with those people who say I should go back to the Philippines, or as they put it, "Just go back to where you came from." When I first came here I was a national but now I'm a citizen. If I go back now I would be an alien because the Philippines is already an independent country and I'm a citizen of another. My feelings towards the Philippines are of course conditioned by my attachment to my own people. The Philippines is important to me but so is the United States.

I always try to respect the interests of other people. I think that the other parts of the world are just as important as the Philippines or the United States. Therefore, I feel I belong to the world. I hold no grudge to any nationality or race because I respect the differences between people through their cultures, and I think all efforts, energies, and money should be concentrated to serving the people instead of making profits for a select group or country here or there. I consider myself an internationalist. You know, I'm proud of the fact that one of the things I got from being in the UFW was meeting people and making friends with people all over the world. Because of the union I was able to travel to Europe. If I go to England, France, Germany, or Japan today, because of the union, I have friends there. For me, that's a nice feeling.

And just because I have left the union it won't change any of this. I still consider those in the union as my friends and those friends outside the union, that I made through my union activities, as my friends. But those who have made the UFW and Cesar more important than life itself I feel have made a big mistake. When you're in the union the world is seen too much as "us versus them." This attitude I think comes from having to constantly struggle for your survival. But now that I have left the union, I really feel so liberated. I see the union as part of my life but not as my whole life. My life within the union, my life now outside the union, are all one: my continual struggle to improve my life and the lives of my fellow workers. But our struggle never stops. When you are older, like I am now, you do want to sit down and rest a little more, but for me that's the only difference.

"A golden foundation"

Authors' Note: In 1987, Philip Vera Cruz was awarded the first Ninoy M. Aquino Award for lifelong service to the Filipino community in America. The award, presented at the Embassy Suites Hotel in Burlingame, California, included a trip to the Philippines in early 1988 to meet with Philippine President Corazon C. Aquino in Malacañang Palace, Manila. This was Philip Vera Cruz's first return to his native country since his departure in 1926. He was accompanied by his longtime companion, Debbie Vollmer.

❧

When I made the trip to the Philippines, I still had not completely gotten over my disappointment with the union [UFW] leadership. So, I really wasn't feeling that well. My overall impression of my short, three-week visit is one of disappointment also. There were many reasons why I felt this way, many of them beyond anyone's control.

It was so hot and humid and there must have been something in the water I drank when I first arrived, or maybe the different food I was eating, because by the end of the first week in Manila I was feeling quite sick. I remember how shocked I was right away by the poverty that we saw in Manila. I feel that at least in the U.S., poor people have some chance to find a job if they really try, even during the Depression era. But over there, I felt that the economic situation was just so bad that there was simply no opportunity for jobs. There didn't seem to be any future for the poor people. That kind of situation over there really depressed me.

One of the first things I remember feeling disappointed about was the distance I felt from members of my family, especially the young ones—you know, the nieces and nephews who I thought would be interested in talking to me. But during that trip no one really talked to me that much and it kind of hurt. Thinking about this now, I realize that there were several reasons why this was so. It wasn't really just their fault. There were many circumstances that caused it to be that way.

One of them, of course, was that I was not in such good physical shape when we were there. When you have stomach problems like I had, it makes you weak and I didn't have much energy. My main purpose of being in Manila, other than visiting with my nieces who lived there, was to have our meeting with President Aquino. That's why I was able to go to the Philippines in the first place. It was the Ninoy Aquino Award that paid for my trip and sent me there.

Well, unfortunately, no one there in Manila notified us in advance when we were scheduled to meet President Aquino. So that first week we had to just sit around waiting all the time to hear from the President's Office when it was our time to go and see her. This made it very difficult for Debbie and me to relax and spend time with my nieces. We couldn't plan to get together in the morning, or maybe for lunch or whenever, since the President's Office might call and we'd have to go over there right away. Now, you can understand this wasn't the fault of my relatives. They wanted to see me and I wanted to see them, but as it turned out we had to put off getting together until the end of my first week there until after I had met with the President. When I think about it, my nieces were very polite, waiting to see me until after I had finished my business with President Aquino. Of course, I felt that I had to be polite to President Aquino and see her when she wanted but that really hurt me since it kept me away for several days from getting together with my family.

The meeting with President Aquino was okay. It was short—thirty minutes at the most. It was nice. I got to ask her about the use of pesticides in agriculture in the Philippines. You know, I kind of asked her why the Philippines was allowing pesticides that are banned in first world countries, like the U.S., to be used there. I don't think she really knew the answer to that question so it remained unanswered. A few days after that meeting Debbie and I wrote President Aquino a letter thanking her for seeing us but we also took that opportunity to mention our concern about the information we've read about the lack of human rights in the

Philippines. I was surprised because we received a reply promptly. It was prepared by one of her staff. You know, the usual bureaucratic letter, written by one of her special assistants. The letter reassured us that President Aquino was doing everything in her power to make sure that people were being treated fairly under their new constitution. It was nice to get the letter and so quickly, but I don't know, just because they said so in the letter, that doesn't mean they are really doing a good job with human rights.

My family is scattered all around the Philippines now, so to see them we had to pack and go to different cities. It was very tiring for me and I was still not feeling that good. We went down to Mindanao to visit with my brother and his family. I got even more sick when we got to Zamboanga City in Mindanao and had to go to the hospital for three days because I was feeling so weak and my stomach was so bad. Everyone in my family treated us well, the Filipino way. They were always feeding us, making sure our room was comfortable, you know, Filipino hospitality. I really appreciate this Filipino trait, but after being away for so many years and my life having been so different than my family in the Philippines, there was something more I wanted from my reunion with my relatives. After all these years, I guess I was kind of looking forward to hearing from them directly about how they felt about the economic and social conditions in the Philippines. I also had hoped to be able to talk with my family about my life in the United States. But it was very difficult to get that kind of conversation going. I wasn't feeling well and time was short. I was there for a very short period. My family didn't seem interested in talking to me about these things that are so important to me. Their Filipino style was just to be nice to me and make me comfortable. And so I was concerned that my family members, especially the younger generation in my family, didn't understand who I am and the things I stand for.

I was surprised to see the husband of one of my nieces wearing a [late Philippine dictator Ferdinand] Marcos T-shirt when we met. I know I have family members who supported Marcos during his reign, but I guess that's true for most families in the Philippines. I had to remind myself that my brother was appointed judge during the Marcos years, so of course, he had a special loyalty to Marcos. In my family some were pro-Marcos and others were anti. I have a niece who wanted to join the guerrillas in the mountains at the height of the Marcos rule, but her father would not let her. I knew that. But still, I was surprised to see this relative with the Marcos T-shirt. It was only later that some people explained to me about these Marcos T-shirts. He had given out so many of these damn things all those years he was ruling, and Filipinos really love to wear all sorts of different T-shirts, that often having one or wearing one didn't necessarily mean that you liked the guy. Maybe you just liked the T-shirt.

I was, of course, curious to find out how much my family, especially the younger ones, knew about my life in the U.S. I have wondered if they knew why I hadn't married and why I didn't have a family like theirs. I never got a chance to explain to them that I never got married because I always felt that if I had my own family then it would not have been possible for me to support my family back home. I wonder still today if my nieces and nephews, many of them who are now professionals, know that I sacrificed my own ambition to get a college education because I had to keep my brother and sister in school through my working. Maybe they know, I don't know. We just never got a chance to talk about it when I was back there. In the Philippines they don't do things as quickly as we do in the United States. I guess if I had stayed much longer we might have gotten around to talking, but on my trip we didn't get a chance and I wish we had.

I have always really believed in education because I knew that was one thing that could open up opportunities for me. After the war, for instance, I could have benefitted from the G.I. Bill to go to school and, who knows, I could have started some kind of business or become a teacher or some other professional. Well, I missed out on that opportunity because I felt if I didn't go to work, my folks would starve in the Philippines and my sister and brother would not be able to go to school. I knew what kind of life my family had when I left the Philippines and I did not want them to remain that way, ignorant and poor. So I wanted to make sure that my brother and sister would have the opportunity to go to school. I knew it was the single most important thing so they could get ahead and live a better life.

Actually, I feel proud of my family. My brother and sister got good educations and they succeeded in providing their children with a good education. That's important to me because I made it possible for them. Someday, I know, they will learn more about my life and how connected we all have been through all these years, although I didn't return to the Philippines for over 60 years.

If I could inspire one or two young people to be successful by hearing my story—which you know by now is the general story of all early Filipino immigrants to this country—if this one or two young people might turn into someone who could help change history, why that would be good! If somebody is moved by this story to do something to help others, to make a sacrifice, to use his or her intellect for the good of their people, not only people in this country will be affected but also those in the Philippines. If more young people could just get involved in the important issues of social justice, they would form a golden foundation for the struggle of all people to improve their lives.

When I was active in the UFW, I was always more interested in the youth than in the older folks. The union was already being run by older people who I felt didn't have a chance to change because they were trapped by their positions of power. They behaved like monarchs, those leaders. They will stay in power until they die if you leave it up to them. I understand that sometimes there are advantages, of course, to retaining the same leaders over the years. Their experience and knowledge can be valuable. The trouble begins when they use their knowledge and their power to receive benefits only for themselves and not for the people or the rank-and-file members. I saw too much of this sort of thing going on in the UFW while I was there. So I've always believed that the future belongs to the young people. Young people can effect change that sometimes old people are no longer interested in. Change, of course, has to come gradually, but I believe that you've got to keep working with the youth to nurture their ideas and ideals.

A number of people will read this book and may question some of the things I've said, some of the dates I've indicated, or the way I've described a situation or event. The fact is that this is the way it happened as best as I can recollect. Hopefully, the scholars will become more interested in our history as early immigrants in this country, and use stories like mine as tools to help study the broader issues of the farm labor movement in this country. If that happens, then my telling my story will have been worthwhile. I cannot tell you how people who read this story will react to it but I think they will react.

Notes

Foreword

1. Gary Okihiro, *Margins and Mainstreams: Asians in American History and Culture* (Seattle: University of Washington Press, 1994), p. 54.

Introduction

1. Renato Constantino, *The Philippines: A Past Revisited* (Quezon City, Philippines: Tala Publishing Services, 1975).

2. Ibid.

3. Nick Joaquin, *The Aquinos of Tarlac* (Manila, Philippines: Cacho Hermanos, Inc., 1983).

4. H. Brett Melendy, *Asians in America* (New York: Hippocrene Books, 1981).

5. Teodoro Agoncillo, *History of the Filipino People* (Quezon City, Philippines: Malaya Books, 1967).

6. Melendy, ibid.

7. "Anti-Miscegenation Laws and the Pilipino," *Letters in Exile* (Los Angeles: UCLA Asian American Studies Center, 1976).

8. Carlos Bulosan, *America Is in the Heart* (Seattle: University of Washington Press, 1973).

9. William Appleman Williams, *The Contours of American History* (New York: New Viewpoints, 1973).

10. Georges Louis Leclerc de Buffon was a French eighteenth-century naturalist. The quotation is from his discourse on his admission to the French Academy, 1753.

Page 2: Profits Enslave the World

† Philip Vera Cruz's poem was put to music in the early seventies by Chris Bautista. With Chris's hauntingly beautiful music, and Philip's words, the song *Profits Enslave the World* became an inspiration for young Filipino Americans throughout the 1970s. What Decolores was to the Mexican American community, *Profits Enslave the World* was for many young Filipino Americans.

"Still good at sitting down"

1. In his introduction to Carlos Bulosan's *America Is in the Heart* (Seattle: University of Washington Press, 1973), Carey McWilliams wrote that Filipinos easily

fell victim to "gambling with loaded dice, rigged cockfighting, phony raffles, tickets for 'sweetheart' contests, and other artful devices." After visiting dance halls in Stockton, McWilliams wrote that the Filipino men would spend the equivalent of a night at the most expensive hotel in San Francisco in the course of an evening by buying dime-a-dance tickets, "so rapidly did the big, red, overhead rotating lights signal the end of a dance." According to McWilliams, "as much as $2 million a year was skimmed off the earnings of Filipinos and other field workers in Stockton in the way of services, gambling, prostitution, and the like."

"The most important $2 in my life"

2. According to Emory S. Bogardus' "Anti-Filipino Race Riots: A Report Made to the Ingram Institute of Social Science of San Diego" (San Diego, Ingram Institute, May 15, 1930), such riots occurred in Yakima, Washington, in 1928; Hood River and Banks, Oregon, Imperial Valley and Exeter in 1930; and Lake County, California, in 1939. *The Evening Pajaronian*, a Filipino newspaper in Watsonville, California, carried this headline on January 23, 1930: "Wild Rioters Murder Filipino in Fourth Night of Mob Terror." The next day, the *Watsonville Registrar* reported, "Near midnight a carload of rowdies drove to the (Murphy) Ranch and began firing into it. The unfortunate men (or boys) trapped like rats were forced into a closet where they huddled and prayed. . . . It was discovered that a heavy bullet, tearing through the walls and a door of the bunkhouse had pierced Tobera's heart." Fermin Tobera's body was sent back to the Philippines. A National Humiliation Day was declared and it was reported that 10,000 Filipinos turned out for the funeral which was sponsored by the Philippine government. The Philippine press referred to Tobera as a "martyr of American intolerance." *Los Angeles Times* columnist Harry Carr wrote on January 31, 1930: "Mobbing Filipinos is becoming an entertaining form of popular amusement. The reason for this is that they are mostly scared little boys who can't fight back. It was a great mistake that the police of Watsonville did not deal adequately with the first mob who started this merry ruffianism. That would have ended it right there."

3. According to Stuart Jamieson's *Labor Unionism in American Agriculture* (Washington, D.C.: Department of Labor Report, Bulletin #836, 1945), "Filipinos were recruited for agricultural labor in California when it appeared that Mexican immigration would be restricted during the 1920s. They were regarded as the sole remaining substitute in the field of cheap labor. . . . It appeared that they were introduced in order to add one more racial element to an already heterogeneous occupational group and thus further discourage possible unionization."

And in *Facts About Filipino Immigration Into California*, Special Bulletin #3 (Sacramento: California State Department of Industrial Relations, 1930), "At times the growers prefer to have the contractor employ a mixture of laborers of various races, speaking diverse languages, and not accustomed to mingling with each other. This practice is intended to avoid labor trouble which might result from having a homogeneous group of laborers of the same race or nationality. Laborers speaking different languages and accustomed to diverse standards of living and habits are not as likely to arrive at a mutual understanding which would lead to strikes or other labor troubles during harvesting season, when work interruptions would result in serious financial losses to the growers."

"I sacrificed too much . . ."

4. The UFW headquarters is housed in a converted tuberculosis hospital: "Nuestra Señora de la Paz," in Keene, California, in the Tehachapi Mountains just east of Bakersfield. Known in UFW circles simply as "La Paz," it is about a one-and-a-half hour drive from Delano.

"A minority within a minority"

5. *Facts About Filipino Immigration Into California.*

6. Carey McWilliams wrote in the introduction to Carlos Bulosan's *America Is in the Heart*: "Filipinos were exploited by the older and better established Chinese and Japanese communities, but their worst exploiters, perhaps, were the Filipino labor contractors whom the growers used to recruit, transport, train, house and feed Filipino field workers. The contractors in the fields and in the fish canneries overcharged, underpaid, and in other ways, ingeniously exploited Filipino immigrants. The labor contractors often brought high-priced prostitutes to labor camps in the asparagus fields near Stockton in auto trailers."

Former California Governor Clement C. Young's *Fact Finding Commission* in 1931, wrote in their report about the role of labor contractor: "Crop owners entered into an agreement with the contractor for harvesting the crop. The contractor, in turn, hired the harvest laborers and paid their wages from money advanced by the owner after deducting varying percentages for his own use. . . . In addition, it has been the custom for the owner to withhold 25 percent of the total wages due until the harvesting was completed when this final lump-sum was handed over to the contractor for distribution to the workers to whom it was due. In many instances, dishonest labor contractors faded from the scene with the entire amount, leaving the workers destitute and without funds to carry them on to the next available job."

7. Philip Vera Cruz, "Racism in Agriculture," *The Catholic Worker* 36:6 (August 1970).

Notes

"The movement must go beyond its leaders"

8. Michael Yates, "A Union Is Not a Movement," *The Nation* (November 19, 1977). Other articles on the controversial leadership of Cesar Chavez: Jack Anderson, "Chavez's Iron Rule," *San Francisco Chronicle* (March 12, 1980); and "Cesar Chavez and His Union Empire," *Washington Post* (March 8, 1980).

"Pounding me with their anger"

9. Philip Vera Cruz, "A Farmworker's Viewpoint" (May 1970); "Racism in Agriculture" (July-August, 1970); "The Farmworkers and the Church" (September 1970) in *The Catholic Worker*.

10. Vera Cruz, "A Farmworker's Viewpoint."

A Selected Bibliography

Carlos Bulosan. *America Is in the Heart, A Personal History* (Seattle: University of Washington Press, 1973); originally published in 1943.

Renato Constantino. *A History of the Philippines: From the Spanish Colonization to the Second World War* (New York: Monthly Review Press, 1975).

Fred Cordova. *Filipinos: Forgotten Asian Americans, A Pictorial Essay, 1763-1963* (Dubuque, Iowa: Kendall/Hunt Publishing Co., 1983).

Arleen de Vera. "An Unfinished Agenda: Filipino Immigrant Workers in the Era of McCarthyism: A Case Study of the Cannery Workers and Farm Laborers Union, 1948–1955." M.A. thesis, University of California, Los Angeles, 1990.

Howard De Witt. *Violence in the Fields: California Filipino Farm Labor Unionization During the Great Depression* (Saratoga: Century Twenty-One Publishing, 1980.)

——. *Anti-Filipino Movements in California: A History, Bibliography, and Study Guide* (San Francisco: R and E Research Associates, 1976).

"Filipinos in American Life." *Amerasia Journal* 13:2 (1986–87).

Emma Gee et al., eds. *Counterpoint: Perspectives on Asian America* (Los Angeles: UCLA Asian American Studies Center, 1976).

Gidra 1970–1990. The 20th Anniversary Edition (Los Angeles: Gidra, 1991).

Hyung-Chan Kim and Cynthia Mejia, eds. *The Filipinos in America, 1898-1974: A Chronology and Fact Book* (New York: Oceana Publications, 1976).

Sam Kushner. *Long Road to Delano* (New York: International Publishers, 1975).

Bruno Lasker. *Filipino Immigration to Continental United States and Hawaii* (New York: Arno Press and the New York Times, 1969).

Carey McWilliams. *Brothers Under the Skin* (Boston: Little, Brown, and Co., 1964).

——. *Factories in the Field* (Hamden: Archon Books, 1969).

A Selected Bibliography

Brett H. Melendy. *Asians in America: Filipinos, Koreans, and East Indians* (Boston: Twayne Publishers, 1977).

Royal F. Morales. *Makibaka: the Pilipino American Struggle* (Los Angeles: Mountainview Publishers, Inc., 1974).

J.A. Pido. *The Pilipinos in America: Macro/Micro Dimensions of Immigration and Integration* (New York: Center for Migration Studies, 1986).

Fred Poole et al. *Revolution in the Philippines: The U.S. in a Hall of Cracked Mirrors* (San Francisco: McGraw-Hill Book Co., 1984).

Mark E. Pulido, ed. "The Puro Pinoy Issue." *Pacific Ties, The Asian Pacific Islander Newsmagazine of UCLA* (June 1990).

Jesse Quinsaat, ed., et al. *Letters in Exile: An Introductory Reader on the History of Pilipinos in America* (Los Angeles: UCLA Asian American Studies Center, 1976).

Daniel B. Schirmer et al. *The Philippines Reader: A History of Colonialism, Neo-Colonialism, and Dictatorship* (Boston: South End Press, 1987).

Amy Tachiki, ed., et al. *Roots: An Asian American Reader* (Los Angeles: UCLA Asian American Studies Center, 1971).

Ronald Takaki. *Strangers from a Different Shore: A History of Asian Americans* (Boston: Little, Brown, and Co., 1989).

Roberto V. Vallangca. *Pinoy 1st Wave* (San Francisco: Strawberry Hill Press, 1977).

Caridad Concepcion Vallangca. *The Second Wave, Pinoy and Pinay, 1945-65* (San Francisco: Strawberry Hill Press, 1987).

Authors Craig Scharlin and Lilia Villanueva with Philip Vera Cruz in Agbayani Village, Delano, California, 1993

CPSIA information can be obtained at www.ICGtesting.com
Printed in the USA
BVOW04s1127221014

371888BV00001B/24/P